Aeschylus: S

DUCKWORTH COMPANIONS
TO GREEK AND ROMAN TRAGEDY

Series editor: Thomas Harrison

DUCKWORTH COMPANIONS
TO GREEK AND ROMAN TRAGEDY

Aeschylus:
Seven Against Thebes

Isabelle Torrance

Duckworth

First published in 2007 by
Gerald Duckworth & Co. Ltd.
90-93 Cowcross Street, London EC1M 6BF
Tel: 020 7490 7300
Fax: 020 7490 0080
inquiries@duckworth-publishers.co.uk
www.ducknet.co.uk

A catalogue record for this book is available
from the British Library

ISBN 978 0 7156 3466 0

Typeset by e-type, Liverpool
Printed and bound in Great Britain by
MPG Books Ltd, Bodmin, Cornwall

Contents

For

AARON RYAN

In am an ghá is ea braitear an cara.

Acknowledgements

I am delighted to acknowledge the encouragement and insight of several colleagues. Alan Sommerstein kindly gave me access to the draft of his forthcoming text and translation of *Seven Against Thebes*, part of the new Aeschylus volumes for the Loeb Classical Library, due to be published soon after the appearance of this Companion. The translation will subsequently be republished in the widely available Penguin Classics series, and is the recommended translation to accompany this volume. Other translations are discussed in the Guide to Further Reading. Professor Sommerstein also generously read a draft of Chapters 1-4, making several perceptive suggestions and saving me from more than a few infelicities of expression. To other colleagues on the Nottingham 'Oath Project', Dr Andrew Bayliss and Ms Kyriaki Konstantinidou, I am grateful for, respectively, fruitful discussion of the ephebic oath and its possible implications for this play, and valuable feedback on Chapter 3. Thanks are also due to Prof. Alexandra Pappas for referring me to bibliography on eye-cups, to the anonymous reader for their suggestions, and to the School of Humanities at the University of Nottingham, who covered the expenses of reproducing images. At Duckworth, Deborah Blake has been a gem to work with, extremely efficient and responsive, and the support of the series editor, Tom Harrison, has similarly been greatly appreciated.

List of Illustrations

1

Play and Trilogy

The *Seven Against Thebes*, also called *Septem* (from its Latin name *Septem contra Thebas*), or, as throughout this volume, simply *Seven*, is one of our earliest surviving tragedies. First performed in 467 (BC), it is pre-dated only by Aeschylus' *Persians* of 472 from among the extant plays, and is one of only seven surviving tragedies attributed to Aeschylus, who is estimated to have written over eighty plays in his lifetime.[1] The authenticity of one of these, *Prometheus Bound*, is disputed. It becomes clear, then, that *Seven* is a rare example both of tragedy in its early form and of Aeschylean craftsmanship.

The context of Athenian drama

The play was produced at the City Dionysia in Athens, an annual festival held in the theatre of Dionysus, in his honour as, among other things, patron god of drama. The festival took place over five days in the Greek month of Elaphebolion, which would be late March or early April on our calendar. The festivities had both religious and civic dimensions, but the sequence of events for the Dionysia and the frequency with which different civic ceremonies were performed remain extremely hazy. There certainly appears to have been a ritual procession, and available evidence suggests that the pouring of libations by the ten Athenian generals was a constant feature of the Dionysia already in existence at the time when *Seven* was performed.[2] The timing of the festival in the spring was doubtless designed to encourage visitors when travel was easier than in winter, and the dramatic festival itself was an opportunity for

9

the demonstration of Athenian prestige and power in the Greek world.[3]

There are several features of ancient drama which are generally alien to a modern theatre-goer, and are worth noting. Theatre in classical Athens was an event in which all participated, with attendance numbers thought to have reached between fourteen and seventeen thousand at the City Dionysia.[4] Producing drama, in keeping with the Athenian agonistic spirit, was a competitive venture. Each year, three tragedians competed with three tragedies and a satyr-play each (on which see below), and five comic poets competed with one comedy each. These plays were appraised by a panel of judges and ranked accordingly. Aeschylus won first prize for his tetralogy of which *Seven* was a part.[5] Theatre was an outdoor affair with no possible lighting effects. One of the major components of Greek tragedy is the Chorus, a group of between twelve and fifteen characters who sang and danced in unison, their songs creating interludes between the action on a structural level, but with a content always of thematic importance to the drama. All actors, including the Chorus members, were male, regardless of their character's gender, and the choral odes of Greek tragedy were accompanied by an *aulos* player. This instrument corresponds to a double-reeded pipe. The Chorus typically remain on stage from their entry song until the end of the play, acting as internal spectators to the drama.[6] The functions of the Chorus in *Seven* will be addressed in detail in Chapter 5.

The tragic trilogy: *Laius, Oedipus, Seven*

Seven is the last and only surviving play in a connected tragic trilogy based on the fortunes of the House of Thebes across three generations. It seems to be a feature of early tragedy, or at least Aeschylean tragedy, to produce connected tragic trilogies. This was not common practice among Aeschylus' successors, Sophocles and Euripides. From the surviving plays, there is only one extant example of a connected trilogy, Aeschylus' *Oresteia* (*Agamemnon, Libation-Bearers, Eumenides*), but of surviving

1. Play and Trilogy

The dynastic genealogy of Thebes

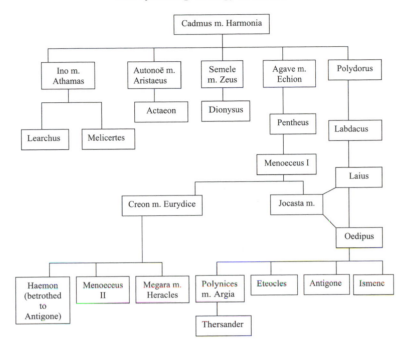

Aeschylean plays, only *Persians* is not part of a connected tragic trilogy.[7] The *Oresteia* makes it clear that Aeschylus consciously developed themes and imagery over the course of the three plays in his connected trilogies in a very detailed and significant manner. Themes such as gender-relations and justice are integral to the *Oresteia*, while complex systems of imagery are exploited including nets, the colour red, and snakes. In attempting to understand *Seven*, we must bear in mind that it was originally intended to function within such a framework. Although *Seven* can stand on its own as a drama (as can each of the plays of the *Oresteia*), some of the subtleties developed in the previous plays of its trilogy are irretrievably lost to us. In a sense, however, we are fortunate in having the last play of the trilogy, as this should represent the culmination of themes and imagery. Furthermore, there is enough which can be gleaned from indications within *Seven* itself, and from fragments of the previous two plays in the trilogy, to cast some light on their content. What follows is a probable sketch of events.

In the background to the trilogy, Oedipus' father Laius receives an oracle from Apollo three times that he must die without offspring if Thebes is to be saved (*Seven* 745-9). The birth of Oedipus thus represents Laius' direct transgression against the oracle which Laius tries to remedy by exposing the child. A detail which we can deduce from a fragment of *Laius* (122) is that the infant Oedipus was apparently left in a cooking pot to die, but he was saved and adopted, growing up in ignorance of his true parentage. *Laius* presents the title character leaving Thebes to go on some journey. After an altercation with a stranger he meets on the way, he is killed, but the stranger is, in fact, Oedipus, unaware that Laius is his biological father. A further detail in the story is that of a murderer (presumably Oedipus) who tasted and spat out his victim's blood (*Laius* fragment 122a), an apparent attempt to avoid pollution. Oedipus then comes to Thebes and saves it from the Sphinx by solving her riddle (i.e. what animal can have two feet or three feet or four feet?), with the answer 'man' (who goes on all fours in infancy, on two legs in adulthood and needs a third 'leg' – a stick – to walk in old age). He becomes ruler of Thebes as his reward, marrying the queen, unaware that she is his biological mother.[8]

In the second play, *Oedipus*, the title character is probably an old man, like Oedipus in Sophocles' *Oedipus at Colonus*, who curses his sons because of their disregard for his welfare and maintenance (implied by *Seven* 786).[9] During the course of the play, he has uncovered the truth of his incest, put out his eyes in horror and cursed his sons. When he dies, Eteocles takes control of the kingdom, and Polynices goes into exile. It is not clear exactly how this happens, but it is evidently unjust, and Eteocles has dreams about the division of their property by a Scythian stranger, only discovering what these really mean at the end of *Seven* (evident from 710-11).

So much can be reasonably deduced, and such glimpses of the previous two plays confirm the importance of certain themes in the third. In Aeschylus, those who commit crimes do not escape retribution. Laius dies because of his defiance of Apollo's oracle. Similarly, if Oedipus is the one who tastes Laius' blood and spits it out, his attempt at warding off persecution is futile, and the crimes of Laius will continue to reverberate through three generations. The disastrous cycle has been set in motion and the third play brings to fulfilment Oedipus' curse upon his sons. The 'Scythian stranger' who will divide the inheritance is iron, a metal thought to have been first forged in Scythia (*Seven* 727-30, 941-3).[10]

The satyr-play

The satyr-play, performed after the three tragedies, is a genre which does not correspond to anything readily recognizable today. It was a lower-style form of drama than tragedy, burlesque in type, and was defined by its Chorus of boisterous and mischievous satyrs, creatures who have the upper body of a man but with grotesque features, and the lower body of an animal (usually a horse in the classical period, though later representations combine man and goat). Only one satyr-drama survives in its entirety, Euripides' *Cyclops*. Several fragmentary satyr-dramas also survive, and from these we can deduce some generic features of the genre. The plays are significantly shorter than tragedies and are thematically concerned with issues like the servility or liberation of the satyrs, divine and heroic infants, sex, new inventions, and athletics.[11] The satyr-play which followed the Aeschylean trilogy of which *Seven* was the final play, entitled *Sphinx*, is connected to the Theban saga which the trilogy dramatizes. *Sphinx* seems to have dramatized an attempt by the satyrs to solve the Sphinx's riddle, driven by greed for the reward if they succeed. The drama is apparently illustrated on a vase-painting showing the Chorus of satyrs as Theban elders listening to the Sphinx's riddle.[12]

The action of *Seven*

As we stand at the beginning of *Seven* we are in the midst of a spiralling cycle of catastrophes, aware of the ominous curse of Oedipus on his sons, and in the knowledge that these two have fallen out over the kingdom of Thebes. The play has been called 'one of the great "battle plays" of Western literature',[13] and rightly so, but this does not mean that the play contains a great deal of what we would call 'action'. Indeed, conventions of the ancient theatre meant that 'battle-scenes' were completely out of the question in ancient drama, partly because violence on stage was generally avoided,[14] but also because of limitations on the number of actors with speaking parts. Tragedy is generally believed to have been born in the sixth century BC, as a development from choral song and dance, when a separate actor was introduced to engage with the choral group. Aeschylus is credited with introducing the second actor, Sophocles the third. If we discount the inauthentic ending of *Seven* (discussed below), the play, as an example of early drama, conforms to the two-actor rule, with no more than two actors speaking in any one scene, though these can, of course, play several different characters. If the Scout from the beginning of *Seven* is the same character as the later Messenger who relates the death of the brothers, this drama is unique in having just two speaking parts overall, Eteocles and the Scout.[15] A further feature of early tragedy evident in *Seven* is the major role of the Chorus, exemplified by the significant number of lines it is assigned.

So, there is not as much 'action' as a modern audience might expect, but there are nonetheless actions which become extremely significant. The issue of the construction of space in tragedy has been important in the treatment of ancient dramatic production.[16] It has been suggested that *Seven* presents an opposition between circular space (outside the encircling walls with the attackers' circular shields) and linear space (inside).[17] We have no stage directions for any ancient Greek dramas, but significant actions tend to be reflected in the words of the characters, and it is reasonable to conjecture how a play was staged, though nebulous areas and ultimately unanswerable questions remain. For example, tragic characters will draw attention to the entrances and exits of characters, a convention clearly derived from the massive scale of the theatre where the actors could be at a significant distance from the spectators. Taplin's influential study of Aeschylean stagecraft uses this convention as its starting point. It is clear that *Seven* does not require the *skênê* building (a fixed structure representing a palace, temple, tent, or interior of some kind), which became indispensable to later tragedy, even later Aeschylean tragedy. In *Seven*, as in the earlier *Persians*, and also probably the later *Suppliant Women*, all entrances and exits can be made through the *eisodoi* (the long side entrances), and it is believed that the fixture of the *skênê* was a later development.

The play opens with Eteocles rallying his male citizens, both old and young, to defend the city (1-38). These are gathered in the *orchêstra*, the circular area which served as performance space for the Chorus and actors.[18] There are statues of the gods positioned on a mound in the orchestra (called an 'acropolis' at 240). Eteocles relays the prophet's divination concerning the attack on the city that very night and encourages the men to think of victory, ordering them to take up positions of defence, at which point they leave. A Scout now appears with news for Eteocles of the enemy camp (39-68). He gives a terrifying description of the seven attacking champions swearing an oath to sack the city or die in the attempt. He witnesses each of the champions being assigned by lot to one of the seven gates of Thebes. The Scout advises Eteocles that a full-scale assault is upon them, and that appropriate measures for defence need to be taken. The Scout leaves, vowing to keep bringing reports, and Eteocles prays to the gods for aid and leaves, evidently to make further arrangements for the city's defence (69-77).

Here, the Chorus of Theban maidens enter, panic-stricken and in disorder (78-180). They hear the din of horses and armour, see the dust rising in the air, and give generally vivid descriptions of the terror provoked by the sounds of the attacking horde. Such references to the oncoming attackers are interspersed with desperate prayers for the city's salvation. The Chorus address each god in turn, and adorn the statues of the gods with the garlands that they have brought as offerings. The effect is unsettling. Eteocles is furious with them on his return, and despises their shrieking (181-202). He orders them to stop causing panic among the citizens and to return indoors where they belong. Anyone who disregards his authority, says Eteocles, will be stoned. An exchange ensues between Eteocles and the Chorus (203-86). They attempt to explain the cause of their panic. Eteocles' responses urge them to pray for victory instead of assuming that the city will fall. Ultimately, he convinces them to be quiet. Eteocles is pleased by their silence and invokes the gods in a manner which he suggests the chorus should imitate. He then leaves to choose six men to station at the city's gates, with himself as the seventh.

The Chorus, left alone, fail to follow Eteocles' advice (287-374), although the first word of their song declares adherence to Eteocles' instructions (287). Their prayers to the gods continue to be based on the possible consequences of subjugation and assumptions of defeat. The Scout and Eteocles return one after the other, and this leads to the central scene of the play (375-682), often referred to as 'the shield scene' or *Redepaare* ('pairs of speeches') after the structure of the scene, which consists of the following pattern repeated seven times. First, the Scout reports on an attacking champion assigned to a particular gate, defined in part by the emblem on his shield; then Eteocles assesses the champion and posts an appropriate defender to meet him; finally the Chorus pray for a Theban victory or the death of the attacker.

There has been some speculation among scholars as to whether or not the Theban champions are present on stage during this scene, each dispatched in turn. However, the great early twentieth-century German Classicist Wilamowitz, followed by more recent scholars such as Winnington-Ingram and Sommerstein, demonstrated that the tenses used in each of Eteocles' speeches make it clear that some of the champions have already been dispatched. It would seem, therefore, that the champions are not on stage with Eteocles when he returns. The champions are matched as follows:

First gate (Proetid Gate): the attacking champion is Tydeus. 'Against Tydeus', Eteocles says, 'I *shall post* the trusty son of Astacus' (407-8) (i.e. Melanippus).

Second gate (Electran Gate): the attacking champion is Capaneus. 'Against him', says Eteocles, '*has been posted* a fiery spirit, powerful Polyphontes' (447-8).

Third gate (Neïstan Gate): the attacking champion is Eteoclus. Against him, 'Megareus *has been sent* whose hands are his boast' (473-4).

Fourth gate (Gate of Athena Onca): the attacking champion is Hippomedon. 'Hyperbius *was chosen* as the man to match this one' (504-5).

Fifth gate (North Gate): the attacking champion is Parthenopaeus. Actor is the man who '*is* to face this Arcadian' (553-4).

Sixth gate (Homoloïd Gate): the attacking champion is Amphiaraus. 'Against him', says Eteocles, 'we *shall post* ... powerful Lasthenes' (620-1).

Seventh gate (Seventh): it is now clear that Eteocles has left only himself from the champions to post at the seventh gate. The scene reveals what is now inevitable. The attacking champion is, of course, Polynices, Eteocles' brother. The Scout exits after his last report (652) and leaves Eteocles to react to the news. Eteocles decides: 'I *shall go* and face him myself' (672-3).

The change of tenses used by Eteocles during this scene is striking and deliberate. The gates form a circle, with Gate 7 next to Gate 1. So we have one block of past tenses and one of future tenses with a single present tense in between. It becomes clear that Polyphontes, Megareus, and Hyperbius have already been assigned to Gates 2, 3, and 4. Indeed, before his last stage exit, Eteocles had declared his intention to choose six defending champions with himself as seventh. The future tenses make it clear that he has not completed the task and Lasthenes, Eteocles, and Melanippus are chosen to defend Gates 6, 7, and 1 during the scene. The present tense relating to Actor can be interpreted either way and creates a reasonable link between the past and future tenses.[19] The element of choice in Eteocles' decision, especially the decision to face his brother, will be discussed in Chapter 3.

Once Eteocles has decided to take on his brother at the seventh gate he calls for his greaves (675-6). This indicates an epic-type arming scene where the warrior dons his greaves first, then his corselet, then his sword and shield, then his helmet, leaving his spear to pick up last (cf. e.g. *Iliad* 3.330-8). The remainder of Eteocles' armour is not mentioned in the play, but it is most likely that Eteocles continues arming himself during the ensuing exchange with the Chorus, as is indicated by the stage directions in Sommerstein's translation (677-719). Certainly, the image of the Seven attackers arming before battle was popular in ancient art (see Fig. 1).[20] The Chorus try to convince Eteocles not to face his brother in combat, but to no avail. Their worries fall on deaf ears and Eteocles exits embracing his harsh fate.

The next choral ode focuses on Oedipus' curse and its fulfilment

Fig. 1. The arming of the Seven before attacking Thebes; Attic red-figure vase attributed to the Makron painter (early fifth century BC). Paris, Louvre G271.

(720-91). The Chorus continue in the same vein as before, assuming the mutual fratricide of the brothers and dwelling on the horrors of three generations of the house of Thebes. The overall tone is one of fear. Such horror and fear create a strong contrast to the Messenger-speech, which opens emphasizing the good news that Thebes has held off her attackers (792-802). The attackers have fallen at the six gates, but at the seventh the brothers have died at each other's hands. The city is saved, but its princes are dead. This epitomizes, in a way, the tension between city and family which is present throughout the play, and which will be discussed in detail in Chapter 2. The Chorus question the Messenger to ascertain the course of events (803-21), and then break into song, not knowing at first whether to rejoice or lament, but reverting to the theme of the curse and lament. As they sing, the bodies of Eteocles and Polynices are carried on and the lament for the brothers continues (822-1004).

The ending of *Seven* (1005-78)

During the course of the lament, the Chorus announce the entrances of Antigone and Ismene, sisters of Eteocles and Polynices (861-3). But the presence of Antigone and Ismene at the end of the play is almost certainly inauthentic. Thematically, their presence makes no sense in a trilogy in which the threat has always been *complete extinction* of the Theban house, dating back to the oracle received by Laius. It is also highly unlikely in the context of the development of gender relations in the play. The tensions between Eteocles and the female Chorus follow a clear pattern, as will be shown in Chapter 5, and the introduction of two female characters so late in the drama would unsettle the balance of gender relations and the unity of female identity in this play. Textually, the suspect passages show signs of having been written by a weaker poet than Aeschylus.

It seems that the presence of the sisters was tacked on as a later addition to make the play conform to the popular Sophoclean *Antigone* which deals with the issue of burying the brothers, and Euripides' *Phoenician Women* which ends with a similar scene. The ending of *Seven* in the transmitted text involves the entrance of a Herald who announces the decree issued by the people's council that Eteocles is to be buried with full honours while Polynices is to be left to the birds (1005-25). Antigone voices her determination to bury Polynices in spite of the Herald's protestations (1026-53). As one scholar has put it, '[t]he entire scene is a dramatic absurdity'.[21] The Herald just scuttles off after disagreeing with Antigone and gives no indication that there will be any punishment for her actions. This strongly suggests that the addition was made for an audience familiar with Sophocles' *Antigone*. The addition will have satisfied the third actor of conventional acting groups. Without the ending, as we have noted, *Seven* needs only two actors unlike other Greek tragedies which need three.

For these reasons, this volume will follow the majority view of scholars that the ending of the transmitted text of *Seven* (1005-78) is inauthentic, and that the Aeschylean play ends after the Chorus' final lament. Lines 861-74 introducing Antigone and Ismene are included among the suspect passages. If the sisters were present during the lament, it would go against convention for the Chorus to lead the lament and not the sisters, another clue that their presence should be regarded as highly suspicious. Lines 961-1004, sometimes assigned to the sisters, were probably written originally for two Chorus leaders. Lines 996-7, where the sisters refer to themselves, are the only indications of personal involvement and these lines are suspect metrically and linguistically and are also probably later insertions, added to tie the presence of the sisters in more persuasively. Discussion of various aspects of *Seven* will not take into account spurious sections listed above. However, the survival of the play's ending, as well as *Seven*'s relationship with Sophocles' *Antigone* and Euripides' *Phoenician Women*, will be discussed in Chapter 6.[22]

The structure, language, and metre of Greek tragedy

We noted above the importance of the Chorus in structural terms in the sense that they sing odes which form interludes to the action, but there are certain complexities of dramatic and linguistic structures which need to be addressed before the central issues of *Seven* can be tackled. All Greek tragedy is written in verse, and the metrical patterns of ancient Greek verse, being based on duration rather than on stress, do not translate well into any language like English. The metre which most closely approximates to conventional speech is the iambic trimeter, and this is the metre used by all characters in *Seven*. An iambic foot (or unit) is a short syllable followed by a long syllable, written ∪ —. An iambic metron is two feet, written × — ∪ — where × (called anceps) stands for a syllable that can be either long or short. A line of iambic trimeter, as the name suggests, is made up of three metra: × — ∪ — | × — ∪ — | × — ∪ — . Sometimes characters are assigned alternating lines in an exchange, as with Eteocles and the Chorus at various points in *Seven*. These lines are known as *stichomythia* and express an escalation of the pace of dramatic action.

When a character diverges from the trimeter register and uses the complicated lyric metres of song, this indicates a heightened emotional state. The Chorus can use iambic trimeters to speak, but most of their contribution to any drama will be made through the lyric metres of their songs. Each song is itself a structured unit, divided into strophes and antistrophes. These are like poetic stanzas that respond to each other metrically. The antistrophe must respond to the metre of the strophe. Several pairs of strophes are normal in choral songs, and such lyrics are often referred to as strophic. By contrast, astrophic lyric refers to a song whose metrical pattern is so irregular that it does not correspond to any strophic structure. The entry song of the Chorus in *Seven* is astrophic in dochmiacs, highlighting choral panic at the sounds of the army attacking their city. The dochmiac (∪ — — ∪ —) is a metre especially associated with a high state of distress.

The content of lyric metres is typically expressed through dense poetic language, and Aeschylean language is especially laden with metaphor and poetic imagery. Choruses often enter tragedy on an anapaestic dimeter (∪ ∪ — ∪ ∪ —), a marching rhythm signalling the importance of their arrival. This is not the case in *Seven*, though anapaests do occur. Finally, choral lyrics, usually sung in unison, can occasionally split into two parts designed to be sung by two Chorus leaders in response to one another, in an antiphonal pattern. Such is the case in the lament at the end of *Seven*. What follows is a brief breakdown of the dramatic structure and metrical patterns of *Seven*.

- 1-77 Prologue (opening act): spoken by Eteocles and the Scout.
- 78-180 Parodos (choral entry song): 78-150 astrophic dochmiacs; 151-80 two strophic pairs.
- 181-286 First episode (second act): 181-202 Eteocles; 203-44 Chorus sing in three pairs of strophic dochmiacs, Eteocles responds each time in trimeters; 245-63 stichomythic exchange (Eteocles and Chorus); 264-86 Eteocles.
- 287-368 First stasimon (second choral song): three strophic pairs.
- 369-719 Second episode (third act): 369-74 Chorus announce Eteocles and Messenger in trimeters. This is followed by a pattern which is repeated six times: Messenger's speech – Eteocles' speech – Chorus response in strophic lyrics, i.e. three strophic pairs. In the seventh instance, the pattern is broken. The Messenger makes his speech, as does Eteocles, but the Chorus respond in trimeters. At 686-711 the Chorus break into an exchange with Eteocles. Their words form two pairs of strophic dochmiacs and Eteocles responds in trimeters. 712-19 is a stichomythic exchange.
- 720-91 Second stasimon (third choral song): five strophic pairs.
- 792-821 Third episode (fourth act): Messenger and Chorus; 803-10 is a stichomythic exchange.
- 822-74 Third stasimon (fourth choral song): 822-31 anapaestic prelude; 832-47 strophic pair; 848-74 astrophic lyrics.
- 875-1004 Antiphonal dirge: five strophic pairs followed by an epode (a closing strophe which has no corresponding antistrophe).

2

City and Family

The violent and incestuous family history of the descendants of Oedipus, and the fate of the city of Thebes are two serious preoccupations of *Seven*. This chapter will discuss the tension that exists in the play between city and family, where Eteocles is characterized both as the king of Thebes and as the brother of Polynices, and where both brothers are shown to display an unnatural disregard for their bond of kinship. Nautical imagery is exploited to represent Thebes as a ship with Eteocles at the helm. Eteocles' abandonment of his position at this metaphorical helm, in order to face his brother in battle, in turn raises questions of responsibility, also discussed in this chapter.

Terminology of city and family

There are some Greek terms which need to be defined before we can begin our exploration of the relationship between city and family in the play: *polis* (plural *poleis*), *oikos* / *domos* / *dôma*, and *genos* (plural *genê*). *Polis* is usually translated as 'city'. This is the most reasonable translation of the term, but it does not capture all the nuances of the term *polis*. In fifth-century Athens, the *polis* (from which our word 'political' derives) was not only the 'city' in terms of territory, but also the civic and political community in which all citizens (who were males only) had a right and duty to take part. Athens in 467 was in the full swing of democracy, but most fifth-century Greek *poleis* were not democracies, and the Athenian *polis* was unusual in this regard. *Polis* life in Athens included attending and voting in the Assembly on matters of legislation and on decisions which affected the *polis*, military responsibility for the defence of the city, and taking part in communal religious festivals. As we saw in Chapter 1, the City Dionysia, where drama was performed, was one such festival, and there was not a clear distinction between the civic and the religious. Dramatic poetry was not just part of an Athenian festival, it was also, and importantly, seen as didactic. The dramatic poets at Athens were thought to teach the citizens of the *polis* through their dramas.[1]

A *polis* setting in mythical time does not necessarily involve all of the associations of the fifth century, or specifically Athenian, *polis*. Certainly the *poleis* of tragedy are all ruled by monarchs, even though these could sometimes express demo-cratic views.[2] But this kind of anachronism is not uncommon in Greek tragedy, and terms relevant to contemporary Greek society were often imbued with particular significance which would have resonated with an original audience.[3] It is clear from Aeschylus' surviving plays that he was very much concerned with the political.[4] His *Persians* is the only extant tragedy which dramatizes a historical event, the aftermath of the Battle of Salamis. Produced in 472, just eight years after the battle itself, it emphasizes the contrast between the absolute rule of the Persian monarch and the free-speaking Greeks who bow to no leader.[5] In his *Suppliant Women*, set in mythical time, the democratic views of the Argive king Pelasgus are set against those of the monarchic Egyptians.[6] And in the *Oresteia*, refer-ence to contemporary political events can be seen in allusions to the alliance between Athens and Argos and the reforms of Ephialtes in changing the powers of the Areopagus court in 462.[7] When Aeschylus died, his epitaph reportedly recorded only his prowess in fighting against the Persians at Marathon, with no reference to his dramatic victories or renown as a poet. In this context, then, the interests of the *polis* will be seen to be a primary concern in *Seven*.[8]

Often seen as a microcosm of the *polis*, the *oikos*, usually translated as 'house' or 'household', represented the family unit within the *polis*. As the centre for the private life of the citizen, it forms the counterpart to the public forum of the *polis* community. The terms *domos* and *dôma* are poetic equivalents of the term *oikos*, which includes the family itself, its slaves, the physical structure of the house, and all the land and assets that come with it. One's *oikos* or *domos* is different from one's *genos*, usually translated as 'race' or 'clan'. Whereas *oikos* and *domos* can certainly refer to ancestry, they are less specific terms than *genos*, where the emphasis is on generation and procreation. So the *oikos / domos* and the *genos* of Oedipus overlap but stress different aspects of family. The *genos* is the generated family line, which, in *Seven*, necessarily reminds us of the pollution of incest within this line. But the *genos* can also have a political implication in Athenian history in the designation of powerful clans (*genê*). The reforms of the sixth-century Athenian politician Cleisthenes, which distributed power more evenly amongst Athenians, and curbed the influence of the *genê*, have been seen to inform Aeschylus' presentation of the *genos* in *Seven* as 'an archaic relic, a family of dynasts ... endangering the state'.[9]

Polis **and** *genos*

It is generally held that *Seven* falls into two broad parts, the first concerned primarily with the *polis* of Thebes, the second with the *oikos* or *genos* of Oedipus, with the revelation that Eteocles will meet Polynices in single combat at the seventh gate as the turning point (630-76).[10] Nautical imagery in the play has been seen to reflect this, where Eteocles is at first the great helmsman of the metaphorical ship of the city (2-3), but ultimately acknowledges, before going to fight, that he is now sailing with the wind of doom (689-91). There is certainly a shift in focus during the course of the play, but we should guard against assuming a bipartite structure to *Seven* based on this shift. As one scholar puts it, Eteocles 'is always *both* the ruler of Thebes *and* the son of Oedipus'. The play 'resonates throughout in both registers, each voice dominant now in one part and recessive now in another'.[11] Although the terms *oikos*, *domos*, and *dôma* appear more frequently in the second half of the play, the *polis* remains a strong focus for concern. O*ikos*-

related terms are used just six times in the play and only once to refer to the house of Oedipus at 720 when the personified Curse of Oedipus is said to be '*oikos*-destroying'. More frequent, and all in the second half of the play, are references to the *domos* or *dôma* of Oedipus.[12] But this does not mean that a focus on the 'family' is absent from the play's first half. Positive references to the *domoi* (pl.) of the attackers who send tokens home at 49, of Megareus who will adorn his father's *dôma* with booty at 479, of the Chorus who fear their *domoi* being plundered (232, 335, 454, 482), and the application of the term *domos* by Eteocles in 278 to mean the temples of the gods, all contribute to the construction of a healthy and auspicious *domos* context against which can then be pitted the polluted *domos* of Oedipus.

A greater concern than the physical 'house' in *Seven*, however, is the preoccupation with birth and race conveyed by references to the *genos* and related terms throughout the play. The first half of *Seven* sets this up in general terms, designating women as a separate *genos* from men, and reminding us of divine birth, for example. There are an unusually high number of references to gods defined by their birth in this play. Athena, Amphion, and the gods generally are *Diogeneis* 'born of Zeus' (127, 301, 538) and Artemis is *Latogeneia* 'born of Leto' (146).[13] Again, such fine and noble births set up an uncomfortable contrast to the awful birth of Oedipus' sons, which is repeatedly hinted at and becomes increasingly explicit as the fulfilment of the Curse looms larger and larger until it is finally accomplished.

In the trilogy, the conflict between *genos* and *polis* has its roots in the oracle given to Laius: that he must die without issue (*genna*) for the *polis* to be saved (748-9). Disregarding this oracle means either of two things: the *polis* must be destroyed for the descendants to survive or the descendants must die for the *polis* to remain in existence. The way in which Laius is presented as giving in to his individual desire for children, despite the oracle he had received (750-7), is to be viewed negatively against the fifth-century concept of acting for the common good of the *polis*.

Although he tried to retrieve the situation by putting the child to death, he nevertheless knowingly endangered his *polis*, a reprehensible act, which has led to disaster. In *Seven* the presentation of Eteocles, member of the *genos* and defender of the *polis*, is key to the dynamics of these issues.

Eteocles: helmsman of the ship of state

Eteocles' first words, and the opening words of the play itself, are an address to *Kadmou politai* 'citizens of Cadmus', emphasizing both ancestry and state. Thebes was reputedly founded by Cadmus who had killed a serpent sacred to Ares, which was guarding a spring. The serpent's teeth were subsequently sown into the ground, and from these sprang up grown men fully armed who fought and killed each other until there were just five left. These five men, called the Spartoi ('Sown men') were the ancestors of Thebes. Cadmus was given Harmonia, daughter of Ares and Aphrodite, as wife.[14] Because Thebes and Thebans are never mentioned in *Seven*, and the city and its people are always referred to as Cadmean, it is probable that the play's title *Seven Against Thebes* is not original.[15]

Eteocles' address to the 'citizens of Cadmus' is followed by his assertion that he is guarding matters in the 'stern of the *polis*, guiding the helm, with unsleeping eyes' (2-3) and that he must tell them the news of the moment. This is significant because it shows Eteocles as tying himself specifically to the *polis* and presenting himself as its completely dedicated leader and protector. He imagines that his name will be on the lips of every citizen if the *polis* is captured (5-8). He sees himself as alone in the responsibility of the *polis'* safekeeping. Yet there is also an emphasis on community among the citizens. He rallies all men, young and old, to help guard the *polis* and the altars of the gods, and to do this 'for their children, and mother earth, the dearest nurse' (16). This is followed by an extended image of mother earth rearing the citizens as children on her kindly soil, and bringing them up to become her 'shield-bearing inhabitants' (19).

An appeal to children and land is not unusual for a leader rallying his citizens in a *polis* under attack. The Greeks under Persian attack rally themselves with thoughts of the liberation of their children and fatherland, amongst other things, in Aeschylus' *Persians* (402-5). However, such images are unsettling when coming from the mouth of Eteocles, where references to children and mothers remind us of his parents' incestuous union. In a play from which Jocasta is absent (she had doubtless killed herself or died somehow in the previous play), the image of earth as mother is even more pointed. It is an attempt by Eteocles to focus away from his own ancestry and emphasize the common descent of Thebes, reinforced by references to the *polis* and its citizens as Cadmean (at 1, 9, 74), picked up also in the speech of the Scout (39, 47). But in the context of the sons of Oedipus, it is impossible to forget the incest which sets them apart from other Cadmean citizens. Eteocles' opening speech thus emphasizes both *polis* and *genos* and shows him investing all his energies into leading the *polis* while rejecting his own *genos* by attempting to present himself as being of common ancestry with his citizens. Amphiaraus will later use similar imagery of earth and mother to rebuke Polynices, discussed below. Ultimately the images of ancestry, with mother earth as nurse, and their implications for the *genos* of Oedipus will be made horribly explicit by the Chorus at 751-6: '[Laius] begot death for himself, father-killing Oedipus, who sowed the holy field of his mother where he was nourished and suffered a blood-stained race.' The image is only returned to a natural context when applied to the Chorus at 792 where they are addressed as 'children reared by <noble> mothers'.[16] The Messenger will shortly announce the death of Oedipus' seed, and the euphemism of mother earth is no longer necessary.

In his capacity as military leader, Eteocles comes across as a good general. He takes affirmative action to defend his city, urging his citizens to take up positions on 'the upper deck' of the *polis* (32-3), continuing the image of Thebes as a ship with himself as its helmsman. He has also had the forethought to send out scouts to report on the enemy's situation, and is assumed responsible for the defence of the *polis*. The Scout makes this clear when he urges Eteocles with the words 'You, as a good ship's captain, must fortify the city (*polisma*), before the gales of Ares storm down upon her – for the land-wave of the army is roaring' (62-4). The position of 'you' at the beginning of the line is emphatic and places responsibility firmly on Eteocles' shoulders. But trust in Eteocles' abilities is further suggested by the image of day associated with Thebes (21, 66) in contrast to the attackers who gather at night to attack the *polis* (29).

In the next scene (the exchange with the Chorus), Eteocles couches his anger in terms of concern for the *polis*. The Chorus, he argues, are endangering the *polis* with their panic-mongering and desperate appeals to the gods. Eteocles had himself prayed for the *polis* to fare well (4, 8-9, 69-77) but now criticizes the way in which the Chorus of Theban maidens utter their own prayers. The Chorus respond to his tirade by addressing Eteocles as 'dear child of Oedipus' (203). This is the first overt mention of Eteocles' parentage in the play and serves to remind both Eteocles and the audience of his true identity. Eteocles' reply reveals his attempt to ignore his *genos* and emphasize his function as leader of the *polis*, expressed once again through nautical imagery at 208-10. Eteocles, frustrated, asks: 'A sailor can't, can he, when his ship is in distress in heavy seas, find an escape from danger by fleeing from the stern to the bows?' The image of Eteocles at the stern of the ship has already been established, and he consolidates this by presenting himself as a resolute leader unflinching in the face of danger. But the Chorus are not convinced by Eteocles as saviour. In fact, after Eteocles' stage exit, they imagine the defeat of the *polis* at 320ff., and tellingly, on his re-entry, they refer to him again as 'child of Oedipus' (372). The dynamic between Eteocles and the Chorus and their insistence on referring to him by his patronymic show that they do not regard Eteocles as the helmsman and saviour of the city, but as the awful product of the oracle that Laius disregarded.

A *polis* in danger

The terrible threat to the *polis* is clear from reports of the determination of the attackers to sack it. They have taken an oath either to sack and destroy the *polis* or to die and mix their blood with the land (46-8). This is a particularly strong oath statement. The only alternatives are victory or death, evidence of a grim warrior force representing a dangerous threat to the safety of the *polis*. The slaughter of the animal expresses the wish of the attackers to die in the same way as the animal they have slaughtered, should they break their oath.[17] The oath ritual itself will be discussed further in Chapter 3, but we should note here an interesting parallel in classical Greek literature. This is the oath reportedly sworn by the Spartans during the first Messenian War, where they swear not to return home until they have either sacked Messene or died in the attempt (Ephorus fr. 216, Jacoby).[18] The Spartans have a serious personal motive for making this oath. Their attack follows the Messenians' murder of their king Temenus during his visit to Messene to make sacrifices. The sacking of Messene is Spartan revenge, but after ten years of inconclusive war, Spartan women demand that the men come home. Caught by the bind of their oath, the Spartans manage to send men home to their women and keep the oath nonetheless by sending home the youngest men who had joined the expedition after the original oath was sworn, and who, thus, were not strictly speaking bound by it. This parallel highlights the atmosphere of excessive violence and determination amongst the attackers of Thebes, amongst whom only Polynices has a real motive for revenge.

This general attitude is reinforced by the boasts of individual champions. Capaneus says that he will sack the *polis* with or without the will of the gods (427-9), and Parthenopaeus swears by his spear that he will sack the city of the Cadmeans by force (529-32), which, as we shall see in Chapter 3, reflects an arrogant attitude towards the gods. But Amphiaraus questions Polynices' attack on his *polis* and his *genos*. Eteocles' opening speech betrayed a preoccupation with *genos* (the nurture of mother earth) as well as *polis*. Here the tension between the two is intensified as Amphiaraus rebukes Polynices (582) for attacking 'his father's *polis*' (*polis patrôian*) and 'the gods of the *genos*' (*theous tous eggeneis*), as well as (584-5) 'the spring of his mother' (*mêtros de pêgên*), and 'the land of [his] father' (*patris de gaia*). The clear question Amphiaraus poses to Polynices is essentially: what is he doing attacking both his *polis* and his *genos*?

Eteocles' reaction to the report of Amphiaraus is markedly different from his response to the rest of the attackers. He praises Amphiaraus as a great prophet and a wise, just, noble, and reverent man (610-11), and remarkably he employs the nautical imagery, previously reserved for himself, to describe Amphiaraus. He is as 'a virtuous man [who] boards a ship together with hot-headed sailors engaged in some villainy and perishes along with that god-detested *genos* of men' (602-4). The expedition ties Amphiaraus to the other attackers in a common *genos* or 'clan', although he is a good sailor caught among foolish ones. The nautical imagery creates a striking parallel. The clan (*genos*) of attackers is doomed just as is the ruling clan (*genos*) of Thebes. The only difference is that all in Amphiaraus' ship will die, while the ship of Thebes can be saved with the single death of its helmsman.

Duality and inextricability

At the seventh gate, of course, is Polynices, who reportedly calls down curses on the *polis* and also wishes the destruction of his brother. He wishes either to kill Eteocles and die beside him, or to banish him as he himself has been banished (631-8). But there is something strange in these two options. The only choice is between both brothers dying or both surviving. There is no suggestion that one might live without the other, and this highlights the duality of their fate and the interdependence of their existence. This duality will be articulated explicitly later in the play, where there are repeated occurrences of compound words prefixed by *auto-* 'self-', and the mutual fratricides are referred to as *autoktonia* 'self-killing/ suicide'.[19] The brothers are also presented as a unit through exploitation of the Greek dual. The dual is a linguistic form used to designate pairs. So Eteocles and Polynices are a 'pair of blood brothers' (681), a 'double pair of generals' (817) and 'a pair of rulers' (921). They 'lie together' (810) and their fate is 'common to both' (812). Common also is their attitude. Like Eteocles, Polynices stresses *polis* over *genos*. The figure of Justice on his shield claims that Polynices will once again possess his *polis* and his father's halls (647-8). The *polis* is given first place in Polynices' restoration. His father's halls are secondary. This may go some way towards explaining the crux of the play.

Why does Eteocles decide to fight his brother at the seventh gate and how responsible is he for this choice? There are two interpretations offered by scholars. The first, somewhat outdated, view is that Eteocles has no control over the fulfilment of the Curse and is simply driven along by his fate.[20] The second, more convincing, analysis is that Eteocles does bear some responsibility for his actions. The communion of human and divine causation would later be central to Aeschylus' *Oresteia*, and it is not surprising to see a similar presentation of causation in this earlier play.[21] Certainly the curse of Oedipus, a Fury personified, has a significant role in events, but there is no question that Eteocles makes a clear decision to fight his brother. The Messenger makes his report and leaves matters in the hands of Eteocles with the words 'you yourself must decide how to command [lit. 'be ship-captain of'] the *polis*' (652). Eteocles' responds with an opening tone of lament and for the first time himself refers to his own much lamented *genos* of Oedipus, greatly hated by the gods, and recognizes that the curse of his father is being accomplished (653-5). But Eteocles checks himself after this brief outburst and returns to the practicalities of going to face Polynices. The Chorus address him once more as 'child of Oedipus' (677), keeping the *genos* in the forefront of our minds, and plead with him not to go to this battle.

The hope that Eteocles will not 'be roused' into battle is emphasized by compounds of this verb (*otrunô*) repeated at 693 and 698. This suggests that there is, in fact, an alternative path, one in which another Cadmean could go to face Polynices, as the Chorus suggest. But Eteocles refuses to be persuaded. At 690-1 he says: 'let the whole *genos* of Laius run before the wind, consigned to the wave of Cocytus [a river in the Underworld], hated by Phoebus [i.e. Apollo]'. This image has been seen as Eteocles abandoning ship, contradicting what he had said earlier about the inability of a sailor in trouble to flee his position (208-10).[22] But the issue is more complex than this. Here Eteocles chooses to defend the *polis* and reject his *genos*. If the ship has, up to this point, represented the *polis*, Eteocles, who has so far largely ignored his *genos*, is now forced to choose between the ship of the *polis* and that of his *genos*, and to recognize that he is captain of both. In choosing to face his brother in battle he takes control of the fate or 'ship' of his *genos*, and consigns it to death. This image is crystallized after the brothers' deaths. At 854-60 the system of nautical imagery concludes, in a complex choral expression, where the Chorus use nautical metaphors to describe the wind of lamentation in their sails 'plying in accompaniment like oars the regular beating of hands on head, which is for ever crossing Acheron [the river on which Charon ferries the dead to the Underworld], propelling on a sacred mission from which there is no return the black-sailed ship, on which Apollo never treads and the sun never shines, to the invisible shores that welcome all'. The ship of the *genos* has become the ship of the dead, doomed forever. The detail of the black sails recalls a disaster of Athenian mythical history when Theseus set out to Crete to free Athens from the yearly tribute of seven maidens and seven youths sent to the Minotaur. He agreed with his father Aegeus, king of Athens, to exchange the black sail of his ship for a white one if he had been successful in his mission, but forgot. Seeing the black sails of the ship returning and assuming his son dead, Aegeus committed suicide. The black-sailed ship represents irreversible doom.

Although Eteocles had continued to try to steer the ship of the *polis*, once he has made the decision to fight his brother, his doom is sealed. Surging waves are said to crash around the 'stern of the *polis*', which has just a thin stretch of wall for protection (757-65). Since Eteocles has been represented throughout as the helmsman at the stern, the image here foreshadows his death under the crushing power of the attack. A difficult passage of choral lyric a few lines later seems to consolidate this image. After referring to the Curse, the Chorus sing (769-71): 'Among men who earn a living, prosperity grown too fat, leads to the whole cargo being jettisoned'. Oedipus' sons, who neglected his maintenance in old age, have been too interested in their own prosperity. The cargo jettisoned from the ship of Thebes to stop it sinking is Eteocles. But the Chorus also fear the devastation of the *polis* along with the death of the princes. Can the ship survive without its helmsman? The answer, of course, will be 'yes'. A *polis* exists as a community, not as a dependency on its ruler. Ultimately, though 'much buffeted by the waves, the *polis* has let no water into her hull' (795-6). The other six champions have secured the safety of the *polis*.

It has been argued that Eteocles' death can be seen as a sacrifice for the *polis*, an *Opfertod* (to use the German term meaning 'sacrificial death', often applied to this feature in Greek tragedy). Scenarios where a human sacrifice is required to save the *polis* or community are not uncommon in Greek tragedy and occur frequently in the plays of Euripides. The best known is that of Iphigenia who must be sacrificed to Artemis for the Greeks to get fair winds for their expedition to Troy, dramatized in Euripides' *Iphigenia in Aulis*, but also mentioned in Aeschylus' *Agamemnon* (205-46). Victims are always female, with one exception. In Euripides' *Phoenician Women*, which also dramatizes the civil war at Thebes and mutual fratricide of the brothers, Jocasta's nephew, Menoeceus, son of her brother Creon, commits suicide in an attempt to save the Thebes from the seven attackers. This may have influenced opinion on Eteocles, but with no hint of sacrificial vocabulary to describe Eteocles' death, and no obvious evidence for this assumption, there is no reason to see Eteocles' death as a sacrifice of this kind, and the *Opfertod* theory has been largely discredited.[23]

Blame and responsibility

But who is ultimately to blame? Is it Polynices for attacking his fatherland? Or is it Eteocles for making possible the kindred slaughter? There is conflicting evidence in external traditions as to which of the two brothers is the elder. Of course, this may well have been clear from the previous play in the trilogy, but scholars have found support for suggesting the seniority of Polynices in *Seven*.[24] If Polynices is the elder brother, then the kingdom of Thebes will have been his by birthright, and Eteocles has committed a terrible injustice in banishing him. When Eteocles anticipates his clash with Polynices, he imagines himself standing as 'ruler against ruler, brother against brother, enemy against enemy' (674-5). The postponement of 'enemy against enemy' gives a greater shock effect to the mention of 'brother against brother', highlighting Eteocles' disregard for kindred ties of the *genos*. Each reference casts the brothers as equals, and the first common trait mentioned, 'ruler against ruler', suggests that Polynices has at least an equal right to rule. The order of reference is significant. The brothers are first and foremost rulers; the *polis* is most important. The *genos* comes second and is qualified by the enmity that divides it.

The speed with which Eteocles makes his decision is also noteworthy. After the news that Polynices is at the seventh gate, he utters three brief lines of reflection on the terrible fate of his *genos* in spoken trimeters (653-5), not in the lyric form generally used in Greek tragedy to express lament. But there is no hesitation such as we find elsewhere in Aeschylus. For instance, when Agamemnon decides to sacrifice his daughter to get fair winds for Troy, he struggles with his alternatives (*Agamemnon* 205-17). When Orestes must kill his mother to avenge his father, he wavers in his resolve (*Libation Bearers* 899). Eteocles is remarkably unfazed by the thought of killing his brother and Polynices similarly welcomes the conflict. Amphiaraus has blamed Polynices for the expedition. It is little wonder that Eteocles subsequently praises him as a wise and prudent man. But Amphiaraus first blames Tydeus for inciting the campaign, calling him a 'murderer', 'a servant of Phonos' (murder personified), and a wrecker of his *polis* (572-5). Tydeus had fled his native city in Aetolia after murdering one or more kinsmen. He has more motive for inciting the attack than the other champions. Like Polynices, he has married one of Adrastus' daughters and expects to lead an expedition back to his own homeland to regain the throne after the sack of Thebes. Unlike Polynices, however, there is no question of his having been banished unjustly, and though Amphiaraus will turn next to blaming Polynices, it is Tydeus who is presented as bloodthirsty.

When Amphiaraus asks 'What claim of justice can quench the mother-source?' (584), the implication is that, although Polynices is going too far in attacking his own *polis*, he does have a claim to justice. Ultimately, the deaths of the brothers are 'new troubles mixed with old evils' (739-41). Eteocles blindly blames the gods for urging events on to their conclusion (719), discounting his own wish to pluck his brother's life (718). But it is Polynices' decision to attack his *polis* and Eteocles' decision to attack his *genos*, which lead to the threat against both, and it is the curse of their father on his sons which tips the balance towards the ultimate destruction of the *genos*. Human motivation and divine fulfilment, which will be discussed in more detail in Chapter 3, are both key elements in the unfolding of events.

Allotment

The fate of the *genos* is a particular concern of the closing choral lament, and the language of allotment is exploited to describe the brothers' deaths. Instead of their receiving an allotted portion of their father's property, Iron, a harsh distributor of property, divides the brothers' inheritance, allotting them only the piece of land in which they will be buried (727-33, 816-19, 906-14, 941-50). Such references to the division of property, it has been suggested, tie in with a change in Greek inheritance law from a system of primogeniture to an equal division of patrimony among sons.[25] But this is not the only way in which the image is exploited. The attackers against Thebes are each assigned to a gate by a process of allotment familiar from epic poetry. This involves the shaking of each warrior's lot in a helmet to see which will come out first, as expressed at *Seven* 457-9.[26] So, the image of allotment in *Seven* follows a now familiar pattern. As with associations of birth and home in *Seven*, here also the natural and healthy context of warrior allotment is cast against the perverted *genos* allotment that is fated to the sons of Oedipus.

Polis over *genos*

The primacy of the *polis* over the *genos* is clear in the attitudes of both brothers, and, although this is unnatural, it reverses the harmful attitude of Laius who put his *genos* above his *polis* in creating offspring contrary to the divine oracle he had been given. Although different aspects of *polis* and *genos* are stressed variously throughout the play, the two cannot be clearly separated, and both are intrinsically linked through the figures of the brothers themselves until the *genos* becomes extinct. After this, the *polis* continues to be presented as the more significant concern. The Messenger presents his news first as a rejoicing for the salvation of the *polis* and only secondly as the death of the *genos*, and the Chorus follow suit. Once the salvation of the *polis* has been confirmed, the Chorus can turn their attention to extensive lamentation for the *genos* of Oedipus.

The importance of the community over the individual in this play would certainly have appealed to an Athenian audience for whom absolute monarchy was an alien and oppressive form of rule. In fifth-century Athenian literature, Asiatics ruled by absolute monarchs were more often than not portrayed as slavish subjects. The defeat of the Persians by the Greeks in the Persian Wars of the early fifth century, in spite of vastly superior Persian numbers and resources, was explained in Greek sources such as Aeschylus' *Persians*, in part at least, by the fact that Persian subjects were forced to fight (willingly or unwillingly) for their king, while the Greeks fought for their individual freedom with far more motivation.

3

Divine Forces and Religious Ritual

Greek tragedy, as we have seen, is itself part of a ritual, a festival in honour of the god Dionysus. But, apart from this, the content of Greek tragedy is saturated with allusions to and performances of religious rituals: oracles, prophecies, prayers, oaths, curses, libations to the gods or to the dead, ritual supplication, sacrifices to the gods, augury and divination, ritual lamentation, and general invocations of the gods. Theatre was 'the most important arena in Athenian life in which reflection on theological issues was publicly expressed'.[1] Many tragedies contain gods as characters. Aeschylus' *Eumenides* unusually contains a mostly divine cast including Apollo, Athena, and the Furies, and his *Oresteia* trilogy exploits the language of religious sacrifice throughout.[2] *Prometheus Bound*, attributed to Aeschylus, contains only one mortal character among a cast of six divinities and a Chorus of nymphs. The plot of his *Suppliant Women* revolves around the Danaids having taken refuge at the altar of Zeus, assuming the divinely protected status of suppliants in Argos, in order to escape marriage with their Egyptian cousins. Overall, the tragedies of Aeschylus are particularly dense in allusions to religious ritual.[3] *Seven* is especially laden with issues of ritual and cursing, and like many Greek tragedies it explores the question of fate and the extent to which mortals can control their own destinies.[4] This chapter will discuss the role of divine forces in the play and will examine religious attitudes, both on-stage and off-stage, in the context of Greek religious ritual and belief.

Divine presences

The statues of the gods are significant stage properties in *Seven*, and although they do not become the focus for attention until the Chorus supplicate them in the *parodos*, it should not be forgotten that they are constant presences throughout, casting a watchful eye over the action. The gods appealed to through formal supplication in the *parodos* and, we must presume, represented among the statues are: Zeus, Athena, Poseidon, Ares, Aphrodite, Apollo, and Artemis. At each god's image the Chorus prostrate themselves and embrace the statue (92-150). This appeal brings an end to their astrophic dochmiacs and is followed by a sharp break in the form of the choral ode, effected through the terrified shrieks of the Chorus and a shift to a strophic lyric pattern. Hera is invoked in this first of two strophic pairs (at 152), along with other deities already mentioned, but it is tempting to suppose that, given the significance of the number seven in this play (discussed in more detail below), there were seven statues on display, representing each of the seven gods who receive a physical appeal. But this must, unfortunately, remain a conjecture. In any case most of the Olympians are invoked through the choral appeals, and most of these are entreated more than once.

The focus of choral prayer to the Olympian gods contrasts with some of the more chthonic deities, invoked by Eteocles and, reportedly, by the attacking champions in the play's opening scene. Eteocles first calls only on 'Zeus the Defender' (8) to come to the city's aid, but after hearing of the attackers' oath to Ares, Enyo (a minor war goddess) and 'blood-loving Terror', he responds with a prayer not only to Zeus but also to Earth, and 'the mighty Curse and Fury of [his] father' (70-1). Like Earth, a Fury was a primeval chthonic deity, associated with earth and blood, and the personification of Terror with the epithet 'blood-loving' has clear chthonic associations. The Olympians, by contrast, were younger gods. The notion of conflict between chthonic and Olympian gods is something which Aeschylus explores in his *Eumenides* where the

Olympian Apollo clashes with the Furies, but the conflict is ultimately resolved, and throughout the *Oresteia* the Furies are shown to be administering the will of Zeus. Indeed, it has been argued recently that Zeus 'the Saviour' is a symbol of coherence between Olympian and chthonic in the *Oresteia*.[5] In *Seven* the emphasis on war also shows how chthonic and Olympian can overlap.

Ares is an Olympian, of course, but his lust for blood can be seen as a chthonic trait usually associated with deities like the Furies. In fact with most Olympians invoked by the Chorus in the opening ode, a savage aspect of the deity is emphasized. Athena is 'lover of battle' (128).[6] Poseidon is 'lord of horses and ruler of the sea' (130) which, in the immediate context, associates him with the violent descriptions of the attackers' horses and suggests that he is in control of the 'wave of enemies' getting ready to batter the 'ship of Thebes'. Apollo is to 'become a wolf' (145) and Artemis to make ready her bow (150).[7] But the strongest divine presences in this play are Ares himself, god of war, the Fury (personified curse) of Oedipus, and the unspecified *daimôn* or 'controlling power'.

Ares

Even in antiquity, the dominance of Ares in *Seven* was noted. Aristophanes' comedy *Frogs* (1021) presents the character of Aeschylus himself describing *Seven* as a drama 'full of Ares', a phrase said to have been coined by the Sophist Gorgias in response to *Seven*.[8] The prominence of Ares is clear from the *parodos*. In spite of being a deity not commonly invoked by young women in Greek literature, Ares is the first god mentioned by the Chorus. He is presented as the god of the *polis* and is referred to three times in this first choral ode, more frequently than any of the other gods. Ares, of course, has a special connection with Thebes. His daughter by Aphrodite, Harmonia, had been made wife to Cadmus, traditional founder of Thebes. Thus Ares is called 'ancient god of this land', and the Chorus ask him if he intends to betray his own country (104-5).

The question is justified since the presence of Ares is very much apparent *outside* the walls of Thebes.

The attackers have invoked Ares as sanctifying deity over their sworn oath, and the spirit of Ares is presented as breathing through the attackers. The Scout reports that 'there breathed within them an iron-hearted spirit, blazing with courage, like that of lions with the light of Ares in their eyes' (52-3). Ares is later said to have possessed Hippomedon in particular, who becomes a personification of Terror (497-500). The Scout urges Eteocles to steer the ship effectively 'before the blasts of Ares squall down' on Thebes (63-4). The Chorus continue this image by describing the attacking horde as 'a wave of men ... raised up by the blasts of Ares' (114-15). They imagine the burning of Thebes, 'and over it blows the blast of the raging subduer of hosts, Ares, defiling piety' (343-4). They hope that the *daimôn* will 'change the wind of [Eteocles]' spirit, and blow with a gentler breath', but it continues to thrive (705-8), and their pleas that he refrain from fighting his brother are ignored. Similarly the breaths of Eteoclus' mares (464) and the monstrous Typhon on Hippomedon's shield (493, 511) are dangerous and threatening. Words translated as 'breath' and 'blasts' all form part of this connected system of imagery, as cognates from the same Greek root (*-pn-*). This unnatural image of breath as an infectious wind of war, which spells destruction, contributes to the overwhelming atmosphere of the terror of war combined with the ever-present pollution of Thebes, manifest in the incestuous progeny of Oedipus. A function normally associated with life is here presented as a perverted poetic inversion breeding death and disease, and the image only reverts to its normal context in the negative expression of Polynices' death as the extinction of his breath (981). The death of the brothers means that Thebes can breathe easily again.[9]

Ares maintains a strong presence among the attackers, but it is also assumed by the attackers that he is present in Thebes. The shield of Eteoclus is inscribed with the words 'Not even Ares will throw me from these walls' (469), suggesting an anticipation that Ares will defend Thebes. He is not only a god of the *polis*. Ares is also connected to the descendants of the Sown men, whom he is said to have spared (412), and thus to two of the defending champions Melanippus and Megareus. The ubiquity of Ares in this play is unsettling, and it is made clear that Ares is both savage and unpredictable. He is an impious god (344) who 'feeds like an animal on the slaughter of mortals' (244).

Gods in Greek tragedy are generally presented as selfish and often arbitrary. Their punishment of mortals can seem excessive and unjustified, and this issue of divine retribution is important in Aeschylean drama. In his *Agamemnon*, for example, it seems that Artemis demands the sacrifice of Agamemnon's daughter Iphigenia as a pre-emptive recompense for the Greeks' future destruction of Troy. She is angry at the omen of the two eagles feasting on the pregnant hare, a symbol of Agamemnon and Menelaus' anticipated victory over Troy (*Agamemnon* 123-39).[10] But in *Seven*, Ares is *specifically* characterized as arbitrary in deciding the outcome of battles with his dice (414). Ultimately, Ares is held responsible by the Chorus for the deaths of the brothers. The brothers' 'reconciler' (i.e. the sword) is 'not free of blame ... nor is Ares pleasing' (909-10), and Ares is further seen as having caused the fulfilment of Oedipus' curse (discussed below).

The Curse

The Curse and the Fury are one and the same in *Seven*, as elsewhere (*Eumenides* 417). A Fury is the personification of a curse, associated with pollution, madness, and vengeance. She is an ancient chthonic goddess, a primeval power, born from the mingling of Earth with blood from the castration of the primal sky-god Ouranos (Hesiod, *Theogony* 178-85), long before the Olympian gods came into being. The Furies were said to have assisted at the birth of Oath, born of Strife, to be a plague on those who swore false oaths (Hesiod, *Works and Days* 803-4). In literature, they are usually described as grotesque in appearance. In Aeschylus' *Oresteia*, in which they play an important part, they are 'grim women like Gorgons with dark clothing and hair thickly entwined with snakes' (*Libation Bearers* 1048-50). They belong where 'decapitation and eye-gouging and throat-slashing are justice', where the masculinity of boys is spoiled, extremities are amputated and men are stoned and impaled (*Eumenides* 186-9). Greek tragedy is often concerned with the inescapability of curses, which take on the physical form of a Fury.[11] In classical art, the Furies are generally not as grotesque as they are in literature. They are females, often young and winged, but the presence in their appearance of snakes twined around their arms or their hair or both expresses their grim nature nonetheless.

In *Seven*, the Curse will manifest itself as a repulsive figure, though she is not the anthropomorphic figure of the Oresteian Furies.[12] She is a black squall on the house which refuses to leave (699-701), and is called 'black' again after the deaths of the brothers (833, 977; cf. *Agamemnon* 462-3, *Eumenides* 52, 370).[13] She is a 'destroyer of families', 'a goddess unlike the gods', an 'all-too-true prophet of evil' (720-2), and her song is 'unmelodious' (867; cf. *Agamemnon* 1186-93, *Eumenides* 330-2 = 343-5). The Furies are most commonly associated in myth with the destruction of families because they are brought into being by kindred bloodshed, and demand blood for blood as requital. In Homer, the Furies are most often the embodiment of a parent's curse.[14] This leads to a potentially unending cycle of violence. The best-known mythic saga of the Furies' pursuit is that of the house of Agamemnon. He is slaughtered by his wife Clytemnestra, who is cast as an avenging Fury (*Agamemnon* 1580), exacting blood for the blood of her daughter Iphigenia, sacrificed by Agamemnon to get fair winds for sailing to Troy. Orestes, their son, must then take revenge on his mother for the murder of his father to prevent persecution by his father's Furies. But committing matricide causes his mother's Furies to pursue him. The cycle of vengeance can only be broken, as in Aeschylus' *Oresteia*, by an appeasement of the Furies through divine intervention. Because of their grotesque appearance and association with pollution, the Furies are rejected by the other gods in spite of their divine status.[15] Even the Olympians dread their ghastly appearance and associations with bloodshed and violence. Although feared, the Fury is a goddess nonetheless and deserves respect as such. This is indicated by the title *potnia* 'lady' which she is given (as at *Seven* 886), a title that is often used of female Olympians.

Eteocles sees the hateful Curse of his father, as he arms himself to fight his brother. She is sitting close beside him 'with dry, tearless eyes, saying "The gain comes before the death that comes after" ' (695-7).[16] Her words show that his death is inevitable, and she urges Eteocles into battle with the lure of 'gain' before death, implying the gain of an honourable death in battle, or even the gain of killing his brother. The word used here for Curse is *ara* rather than Erinys. Technically the distinction between the two would be that an *ara* is a curse invoked for general purposes, while the Erinys is a curse more specifically tied to kindred blood-pollution. So the 'black Erinys' is the 'shadow of Oedipus' (976-7 = 987-8). But the two are clearly meant as synonymous for the purposes of *Seven*, as made clear at their first mention where they are identified with each other (70). The father's curse is referred to as an *ara* (945) as well as an Erinys, and the two terms are used equally in the play. Indeed, the Curse in *Seven* is naturally a conflation of both an *ara* and an Erinys. Oedipus' curse on his sons was a response to their neglect of him. This curse does not spring from bloodshed. But the Erinys is part of the *genos*. Oedipus' murder of Laius has stained the *genos* with blood pollution, and the incest he commits is presented as producing 'bloodstained offspring' (755). The Curse is first mentioned in the prologue, but does not resurface again until 655. The effect is that the audience are aware of the Curse looming over the action of the play, but are tensely anticipating its manifestation, suppressed for so long. This tension is further compounded by the fact that Oedipus' curse on his sons is so unclear in its terms, in contrast to other versions, such as Sophocles' *Oedipus at Colonus*, where the curse is completely unambiguous, as will be discussed in Chapter 6.[17] The lapse between the first mention of the Curse and its subsequent re-emergence also allows for the development of human decisions which, together with the Curse, drive events to their conclusion.

When Eteocles decides to face Polynices, the Chorus ask him why he is raging madly (686), and plead with him not to be carried away by the 'spear-mad delusion' that fills his heart (687-8). But persecution by a Fury goes hand in hand with madness, the concept being somewhat akin to possession by a demon in Biblical scripture. In *Seven*, the madness is not as explicit as in other treatments of Fury-induced tragic madness. There are no rolling eyes, no foaming at the mouth, no hallucinations such as mark Orestes' suffering in Euripides' *Orestes*. Fury-induced madness in tragedy is usually connected with blood pollution, which the brothers have not yet incurred. But the madness which already characterizes their actions expresses the advent of the kindred slaughter which will ultimately take place. It is also connected with divine possession by the *daimôn*, discussed below. The word translated above as 'delusion' is the Greek term *atê*. This state of delusion in early Greek poetry represents the first stage of madness, a preliminary damage caused to the mind.[18] It is, for example, 'the delusion [i.e. panic] that makes [men] throw away their arms' rather than defend their city (315), and, at the same time, it is the delusion that would make brother take up arms against brother. The brothers, we are told, were 'divinely possessed by Atê' (1001).

Madness is particularly prominent in the second half of the play, as the Curse's fulfilment becomes increasingly inevitable. Oedipus was said to have had a 'damaged mind' (725) and a 'maddened heart' (781) when he cursed his sons. Laius' defiance of Apollo in coupling with his wife is described as 'mindless madness' (756-7).[19] Eteocles and Polynices are 'ill-witted' in capturing their father's house with the spear (875), and they die because of 'insane strife' (935-6). The fulfilment of the Curse is intrinsically linked with acts of madness. Once fulfilled, the grief it causes is akin to madness (919-20, 966). In the lament over the brothers, the Chorus link the Arai 'Curses' with Atê 'delusion' (954-60):

> Over your deaths the Arai have shrilled
> their high-pitched cry of triumph, having put the *genos*
> to flight in utter rout.
> The trophy of Atê stands at the gate
> at which they were struck down, and the *daimôn*
> has defeated the two men and ended its work.

We see here the forces of the Curses, of Atê, and of the *daimôn* working in unison to ensure the destruction of the *genos*. This highlights once again the different levels of causation involved in the fulfilment of the Curse. The Curse itself comes into being as an autonomous creature, but Atê has been responsible too for causing the delusion that accompanies persecution by a curse, and the mysterious *daimôn* similarly drives events to their conclusion.

Like the ubiquitous presence of Ares, the Curse and its madness are also manifest outside the walls of Thebes. Tydeus is called the 'summoner of a Fury' (574), Polynices utters curses against Thebes (633),[20] and the air is 'mad with the brandishing of spears' (155). The horses' breath is said to be 'white foam' which drips and stains the soil (60-1), a suggestion that they too are infected with this mad lust for destruction. This image of dripping and staining the soil is one which is repeated in the description of bloodshed, also directly connected to the Curse. The result of the kindred slaughter of the brothers is that 'the dust of the earth drinks up their dark red clotted blood' (735-7), and no one can provide purification from 'a pollution which can never grow old' (682).[21] There will be no 'pure' conclusion to the war as the Chorus had hoped (162), rather the 'life-strength [of the brothers] is mingled in the earth as it flows with gore' (937-40). The emphasis on the earth drinking the brothers' blood is significant as it represents the appeasement of the Fury. The earth is, in a sense, the chthonic Fury itself satisfying its need for blood.[22]

The *daimôn*

The Greek entity of the *daimôn* is a difficult one to interpret. A *daimôn* is a god, any god. In the plural, the term *daimones* is commonly used to refer to the gods in general (as at *Seven* 77, 96, 173, 211, 236, 515, 823). But the *daimôn*, as a singular entity, can also be an independent spiritual force, typically unpredictable and arbitrary. In a polytheistic religion where each god is patron of a specific area of human life, the *daimôn* does not conform to this pattern. It does not receive cult and is not associated with any particular aspect of existence. It is a non-specific divine force, comparable to the force of fate (*tychê*). Although the word *daimôn* is the source for our word 'demon', the Greek *daimôn* is not necessarily a force for ill. A person who is *eudaimôn*, literally 'with a good *daimôn*', is 'blessed', 'prosperous', 'happy'. A person who is *kakodaimôn*, literally 'with a bad *daimôn*', is 'cursed', 'unlucky', 'unhappy'. The brothers in *Seven* are described with the poetic synonym *dysdaimones* (827), and the mother who bore them is similarly *dysdaimôn* (926). A *daimôn* is a non-descript divine power, and its supernatural force, as it manifests itself in *Seven*, is perhaps best translated, with Sommerstein, as 'controlling power'.

We have seen how the *daimôn* is connected with the Curse in overseeing the unfolding of the fratricide. It is also mentioned separately as the cause for the fratricide, each brother having had the same *daimôn* (812-3). The *daimôn* is further connected with the other central force in *Seven*, Ares. The Chorus refer to Ares as the '*daimôn* of the golden-helmet', which reinforces the presentation of both Ares and the *daimôn* as unpredictable powers. Indeed, the term *daimôn* is only used twice to refer to a specific deity in *Seven*, and each time it refers to a grim or frightening force. So Ares is a *daimôn*, but so also is Typhon (523), the earth-born monster with one hundred snake-heads which breathe out smoke. The *daimôn* as its own entity is associated with imagery of breathing, as we have seen, when the Chorus hope it will change the wind of Eteocles' spirit and blow with a gentler breath (705-8). Part of the danger inherent in the *daimôn* is the inability of mortals to seek its protection or patronage. To know the name of a *daimôn* is to acquire power over him.[23] Because the *daimôn* is unidentifiable, it is impossible to summon the *daimôn* to one's aid. One is simply at its mercy. Thus, when the brothers kill each other they are *daimonioi* 'possessed' (892, 1001).

The oath ritual of the attackers

The divine forces which the attackers call to their aid are unusual. Their oath ritual (42-51) is one of the most solemn pacts in archaic or classical Greek poetry. The slaughter of an animal is common enough in formal oath ritual (sheep are slaughtered as oath sacrifices in the *Iliad*, for example), but there are several grim features of the attackers' oath ritual in *Seven*. The deities invoked, Ares, Enyo, and Terror, are violent and unpredictable, and occur only here in this combination in an oath. There is one other instance in classical Greek poetry of an invocation of Ares to witness an oath. This is the oath of Creon's son Menoeceus in Euripides' *Phoenician Women*, but circumstances there are very different. Menoeceus swears that he will not betray his father, brother, or city before committing suicide in an attempt to save Thebes from the fratricidal war which it also dramatizes. Nevertheless, it is noteworthy that Ares should be present as oath-sanctifying deity in both these plays, and nowhere else in poetry, reinforcing Ares' ubiquitous presence in this episode in the Theban saga.

However, the combination of Ares and Enyo invoked as oath-sanctifying deities also occurs in the Athenian ephebic oath. Admittedly, there, they are only two out of seventeen overseers invoked, but it is interesting to compare the contexts, both of which are military. It is not exactly clear when the ephebic oath was introduced, but if it could be referred to as an 'ancestral' oath in the mid-fourth century by Dio, son of Dio of Acharnae, priest of Ares and Athena Areia (i.e. 'Ares-like'), it is probable that it existed already in the fifth century. Indeed, scholars have seen early traces of the ephebic oath in the works of

Thucydides, Sophocles, and even Aeschylus' *Persians*, which pre-dates *Seven*. It is more than likely that the oath existed in the early fifth century.[24] The inscription on which the oath survives comes from Acharnae, a deme where Ares had a special position, but it is reasonable to suppose that the oath, being military as well as civic, always included him. The epithet of Athena as 'Areia', however, is more likely to be a local addition.

The ephebic oath was taken by Athenian *ephebes*, young men on the cusp of eligibility to military service, aged about seventeen.[25] The oath itself is essentially a pledge to stand united in defending Athens from enemies, and to respect its laws and ancestral religion. The oath of the Seven, by contrast, is one of unity in attack rather than defence, and the attitude of the Seven to religion is overwhelmingly arrogant rather than respectful. The Seven, of course, are far from being *ephebes*, with perhaps the exception of Parthenopaeus, who is one of the most arrogant. But the comparison with the ephebic oath shows that the invocation of Ares and Enyo is specifically militaristic, while the fact that no other deities are invoked in *Seven*, apart from Terror, confirms that the nature of the campaign is purely aggressive. This is just one of many strands which combine to portray the Seven as an extremely dangerous military threat. If the invocation of Ares early on does recall the ephebic oath for an Athenian audience, then it cannot be a distancing device as one scholar has argued.[26]

During the Persian Wars, several sources report that the Greeks had sworn to destroy any cities which surrendered to the Persians. The Thebans who had medized (i.e. defected to the Persian side) would have been included among these, and it has recently been suggested that there are strong reasons to believe that an oath to destroy Thebes had been taken. Indeed, the oath would have stated that punishment of Thebes would take place after the defeat of the barbarians, which happened in 479. In fact, the Theban leaders were executed but Thebes itself was not destroyed, and the oath was apparently ignored because, it is argued, it proved impossible to fulfil.[27] If such an oath had been taken in recent Athenian history, the oath of the Seven to destroy Thebes or die in the attempt takes on an extra dimension of political significance. If the Greeks had failed to fulfil their oath to destroy Thebes in the aftermath of the Persian Wars, then the determination of the Seven might be read as a political comment on the leniency with which Thebes was treated. This is an attractive hypothesis, but, as with many suggestions of political references in Greek tragedy, it must remain speculative.

The blood of the slaughtered bull in *Seven* is caught in a 'black-rimmed shield' (43), and the attackers dip their hands into the blood. This last detail indicates a particularly high degree of solemnity attached to the oath. A comparable solemnity was required in homicide trials, where participants touched the severed pieces of the slaughtered sacrificial animals as a sanctifying feature of their oaths.[28] Elsewhere, parties are occasionally said to dip weapons into the blood of slaughtered oath sacrifices. In 401, an alliance between the Greeks and the Persians is sealed near Cunaxa by slaughtering a bull, a wolf, a boar, and a ram also over a shield. The Greeks are said to dip their swords, and the Persians their spears, into the blood (Xenophon, *Anabasis* 2.2.8-9). The barbaric Scythians, when taking oaths, mix a few drops of blood from each party of the oath with wine and then dip into this mixture a sword, arrows, a sagaris (axe), and a javelin. The two parties then drink the wine and blood (Herodotus, *Histories* 4.70).

There is no suggestion that the Seven drink the blood, but it is clear that the oath ritual in *Seven* was meant to be taken as solemn. Indeed it has been compared to the ritual of offering blood before entering the Underworld, as Odysseus does in *Odyssey* 11.34-98, and the shield has been seen to fulfil the function of the sacrificial cup.[29] Its impact in antiquity is attested by the fact that the ceremony was parodied by Aristophanes in his *Lysistrata*. This involved the 'slaughter' of a jar of Thracian wine over a large, black-based cup. Here the blood is replaced entirely with wine and the pact is a sex strike, but the reference to *Seven* is unmistakable. The oath ritual of the attackers reinforces their savage determination and the terrifying threat to

Thebes, and the power of this scene inspired the 1839 bas-relief sculpture of Théodore Gruyère, who emphasizes the unity of the warriors as they simultaneously place their hands over the oath sacrifice (Fig. 2).

Fig. 2. Gruyère, 'Le Serment des Sept Chefs devant Thèbes', Prix de Rome de Sculpture, 1839, PRS 27. Paris, École Nationale Supérieure des Beaux-Arts.

Theban attitudes to prayer

A striking feature of *Seven* is the contrast between Eteocles and the Chorus in their attitudes to prayer. Eteocles is appalled by the Chorus' motivation in praying, which he sees as excessive fear, and feels that their descriptions of potential disasters will only undermine the morale of the citizens. He persistently tries to silence the Chorus. For their part, the young Chorus-women feel perfectly justified in their attitude to prayer and suggest that Eteocles is not doing enough to gain divine favour. To what extent is an audience expected to agree with either Eteocles or the Chorus? This is a difficult issue to judge. It has generally been seen as 'a contrast between a hysterical female Chorus and a measured male leader', though a minority of scholars have been critical of Eteocles, finding him too harsh, and have been more sympathetic to the Chorus.[30] Much of this debate centres on the different attitudes of the Chorus and Eteocles to prayer. Is Eteocles right in condemning choral prayers as dangerous? Is Eteocles unaware of his own shortcomings in terms of proper piety? A recent and convincing analysis of the patterns of prayer and curse in *Seven* suggests that the answer to both these questions is 'yes'.[31] In other words, there is fault on both sides, a recurring pattern in *Seven*. But as the play progresses, the Chorus act more and more appropriately while Eteocles veers off in the opposite direction.

Eteocles' prayer to 'the mighty Curse and Fury of [his] father' in the opening scene is disturbing not only in the immediate context of the play, but within ancient Greek attitudes to prayer more generally. The Curse and Fury of Oedipus are directed against Eteocles himself (and, of course, Polynices). To pray to a spirit whose function is to destroy him is a remarkably inappropriate action on Eteocles' part. Indeed, it has been argued that the implacability of the Furies means that they are not appropriate recipients of prayer or cult.[32] Of course, Eteocles does not yet understand the true meaning of the Curse. We must assume he believes that the Curse will now attribute to him his rightful inheritance. Nevertheless, it remains highly inappropriate to invoke an inherently destructive power in a prayer for salvation. Even in terms of narrative structure, the appeal to the Curse and Fury comes as a shock, placed, as it is, directly after an appeal to the gods of the *polis*, a phrase which would more normally end a series of invocations.[33] Eteocles will rebuke the Chorus for an inappropriate emphasis on the fear of destruction at Thebes, but his own prayer is formulated in precisely such negative terms: 'do not let my city be captured by its foes, do not uproot it out of Greece, stock and branch, in utter destruction! Never bind this free land and this free city of Cadmus under the yokestrap of slavery!' (71-5).[34] When the Chorus pray in a similar fashion, Eteocles' responses border on the blasphemous. 'Assembled gods, do not betray our walls!' the Chorus pray (251). Eteocles wants them silenced. 'Almighty Zeus, direct your bolts against the enemy!' they pray (255). Eteocles reproaches Zeus for creating the women who pray to him (256).[35]

Eteocles is completely unaware of the inappropriateness of his attitude to prayer, but he does have a valid point in reproaching the Chorus for making potentially dangerous over-negative statements. In Greek thought the expectation of disaster can be ill-omened and apotropaic measures should be taken to avoid such negative speech. A simple example of this principle is evident in the euphemistic names adopted for the inauspicious. The Black Sea in classical Greece was an area known for its treacherous waters, and thus was given the apotropaic name of *Euxeinos Pontos* 'Hospitable Sea' in the belief that a euphemistic name would be likely to appease the sea's hostile powers. Similarly, the left-hand side was thought unlucky in antiquity and was named *euônumos* in Greek, 'the well-named' side, as at *Seven* 887, where we are told that the brothers struck each other in their left sides. Another Greek word for 'left' is *aristeros*, literally 'better'. The Furies themselves were called the *Eumenides* 'the Kindly Ones' in an attempt to propitiate them.[36] The negativity of the Chorus and Eteocles contributes to the ominous atmosphere of foreboding and disaster which is constructed in the first part of the play. The Chorus do finally accept Eteocles' main criticism of their approach to prayer and gradually change their attitude, but Eteocles fails to realize that the same reproach of inappropriate prayer could be brought against him.

Reciprocity and piety

A key aspect of ancient Greek religion was reciprocity, a system in which gods and mortals need each other. Clearly mortals need to offer due worship to the gods to gain their favour, but gods also need to give favour in order to expect sacrifices and worship, a *do ut des* 'I give so that you give' principle.[37] Mortals can, to a certain extent, threaten gods into coming to their aid. In Euripides' *Iphigenia among the Taurians*, for example, Orestes reports how he threatened to starve himself in Apollo's temple if the god refused to come to his aid (974-5), an act which would cause serious pollution. This concept of reciprocity is reflected at various points in *Seven*, including in the traditional prayer formula where the deity petitioned would be given a reason for granting aid. So Eteocles closes his prayer in the opening scene with the words 'when the *polis* enjoys success, it honours its gods' (77). He later invokes the gods of the city, pledging that 'if all turns out well and the *polis* is saved, we will redden the altars of the gods with the blood of sheep, set up monuments of victory, and fix the spoils of the enemy, gained by the stroke of the spear, in their holy temples' (274-8).[38] The dramatic entry of the Chorus is motivated by bringing offerings and prayers to the gods, and they remind the gods of the people's worship and the sacrifices carried out by the *polis* in their honour (174-80).[39] Linked to this concept of reciprocity is the notion that reliance on the gods alone is not enough to save Thebes, and human endeavour must be coupled with divine will. Eteocles implies this when he says that the gods will keep off enemy attack but then muses on the fact that 'it is said that the gods of a captured city leave it' (216-18).

There is one deity, of course, which has not yet received its due sacrifice and is not yet appeased – the Fury of Oedipus. This becomes evident during the Chorus' attempt to persuade Eteocles not to go against his brother. 'The Fury's black squall will leave your house, once the gods receive a sacrifice at your hands', they say (699-701). Eteocles replies 'The gods, it seems, have already abandoned us, and will they honour any gift from us, doomed as we are? Why then should we still cringe before the fate of death?' (702-4). This is an interesting exchange. The Chorus are right that a sacrifice needs to be made, but they do not realize that the Fury will only be appeased by the blood of the brothers. In leaving to fight his brother, Eteocles is actually becoming the sacrifice which will lift the Curse from the house. His conviction that the gods have abandoned him suggests, in the context of 216-18, that he feels the city is doomed to capture. But he is also mistaken. He has confused *polis* and *genos* once again. It is he who is doomed, not the city.

The Thebans overall, whether appropriately or inappropriately, attempt to gain the favour of the gods through prayers and offerings. The attackers, however, are not all so pious. Several can be labelled as blasphemers. Tydeus hurls insults at the prophet Amphiaraus for preventing him from crossing the river Ismenus because of bad omens (377-83). It is made clear in this play that Amphiaraus is a true prophet and a great man, to be admired even by his enemies. Disregarding his mantic powers and abusing him like this is inadvisable behaviour on Tydeus' part, and is likely to invite divine displeasure.

Parthenopaeus reveres his spear more than any god and swears an oath by this spear rather than god that he will sack Thebes (529-31). Swearing an oath on an object rather than by a god is not common in Greek literature, but not unknown. The best parallel is probably Achilles in the *Iliad* (1.233-46) who swears by Agamemnon's sceptre. But the effect there is very different. Achilles is attempting to exercise some control in the power dynamics of the Achaeans by refusing to fight. It is appropriate for him to use the sceptre of Agamemnon, symbol of power over the army, to make his statement. There is no indication that he sees the sceptre as superseding the power of the gods. Indeed the sceptre is used as a sanctifying feature in subsequent Iliadic oaths: by Agamemnon at 7.408-13, and by Hector at 10.321-32. By contrast Parthenopaeus explicitly values his spear above any god in a dangerous way, and his oath to sack Thebes will remain unfulfilled.

Similarly the boast of Capaneus to sack Thebes fails to come to fruition, but of all the attackers, it is he who is most extreme in his blasphemies. He is said to show 'a pride beyond human limits' in his boasts, claiming that he will sack the city with or without the will of god 'and that not even the weapons of Zeus crashing down to earth will stand in his way or hold him back'. Zeus' thunderbolts are, he says, only as strong as the midday sun (425-31). This is not just a defiance of Zeus, it is an outright rejection of his powers. As fitting to his blasphemies he will be destroyed by Zeus' thunderbolt as he attempts to enter Thebes (Euripides is explicit in his version at *Phoenician Women* 1180-1). These impieties are shown to taint the whole group of attackers, even the virtuous, pious prophet Amphiaraus. He has 'become mixed up against his will with impious men of arrogant speech ... and, Zeus willing, he will be dragged down with them' (611-14). In this instance of group justice, Amphiaraus will be laid low by the gods like the rest.

Numbers and naming

In a highly superstitious culture, numbers and names could have special powers in the context of prayer and curse. In *Seven* we see the numbers three and seven have particular significance, numbers which are also considered significant in Biblical scriptures. Like Peter, who denied Christ three times, Laius had defied Apollo three times, returning to the oracle each time in hope of a different answer to his query (746). His ultimate disregard for Apollo's warning caused his sin to remain into the third generation (744-5), which recalls the Old Testament God of Exodus 20.5-6, who visits the sins of the fathers upon the children of the third and fourth generations. The attack on Thebes is a wave (curse) of triple strength breaking loudly around the poop of the city (Eteocles) at 757-60, and the sufferings of the house are 'thrice-brandished' (985). So the number three is significant for the house of Laius as it represents the culmination of its extinction, but it is also important in terms of the play's structure. *Seven* was, of course, the third play in the trilogy, but within the drama itself there exists noteworthy engagement with triadic structures.[40]

It has been suggested that the shields of the attacking warriors can be read in various triadic forms.[41] The first triad of symbols represents a progression from primeval to civilized man. The moon and stars are a symbol of celestial beginnings, the naked man armed with a fire-brand represents early man, and the armed warrior scaling the city walls represents the technology available to the world of heroes. The second triad works in a similar way charting the rise of man in civilization and his relationship with the divine. Typhon is an archaic monster in power before the days of men and subdued by Zeus. The Sphinx, a plague to man, was nevertheless defeated by a man, while the blank shield of Amphiaraus represents his clairvoyance as a divine prophet, fully aware that the expedition is doomed and that no symbol however powerful can alter the course of fate. An element of ring composition closes the two triads off as a unit. The first attacker and the sixth, Tydeus and Amphiaraus, are diametrically opposed, each uttering insults against the other. Viewed as such a structure, the lone figure of Polynices forms, in yet another way, the perfect counterpart for Eteocles.

But perhaps more striking still are the ways in which expected tripartite structures are aborted. Auspicious prayer was tripartite in structure, consisting of invocation, argument, and request. Cultic hymns should be monostrophic or triadic, but the 'religious disarray' of the Chorus' opening song openly flouts such conventions.[42] Here Aeschylus has manipulated and deconstructed a recognized tripartite structure of Greek religious worship in order to underline the terror experienced by the Chorus. Comparable is the rupture in the third strophic pair of the third choral ode (second stasimon), which deals with the three generations of the Curse (720-91). It has been noted that the third strophic pair of the ode is marked by a sharp division causing the ode to be split into two halves of essentially the same structure, in an abrupt transition, with the third strophic pair marking the break from past to present.[43]

The importance of the number seven for the drama is immediately apparent in several ways: seven attackers, seven defenders, seven gates, and possibly seven statues of deities on stage. It was suggested in antiquity that Aeschylus had consciously reduced the number of attacking champions to seven.[44] Another hypothesis suggests that the number seven comes from 'the epic transposition of a purification ritual of ultimately Babylonian origin'.[45] The ritual in question featured seven fierce warriors and seven defenders who conquer their enemies, and twins fighting at a gate. Aeschylus does, in *Seven*, suppress the host in dealing with the attack on Thebes and focuses very much on seven individual champions.

It has also been argued that there are symbolic associations between the seven planets (Sun, Moon, Mars, Mercury, Jupiter, Venus, Saturn) and Aeschylus' seven heroes and gates.[46] Although this is an attractive hypothesis, it is unsupported by Greek astrological knowledge. Greeks did not know that there were seven planets until the fourth century (Eudoxus), or the very late fifth (Philolaus). Before this Greeks recognized only the morning and evening star (Venus) and a 'midnight planet' (Mesonyx), which may have referred to Mars, Jupiter, or Saturn, not clearly distinguished from each other at that time.[47] However, there is one unusual expression in *Seven*, used to describe Apollo at line 802, which deserves special attention here. He is called 'the seventh leader', which is probably an Aeschylean coinage based on a combination of certain epithets of Apollo which refer to him being born on the seventh day of the month, and others which refer to him as a leader.[48] This coinage must surely relate to Apollo's role in causing, even 'leading' the fulfilment of the curse at the seventh gate through his original oracle to Laius which was ignored.

Interestingly, the seventh gate is the only one of the Theban gates whose name corresponds to its number. The importance of a name in terms of ritual and curse is that knowledge of a person's name gives another the power to curse them. This is well known from the *Odyssey*, where, in Book 9 (502-21), Odysseus' revelation of his name allows the Cyclops

Polyphemus to call down the curse of his father Poseidon on Odysseus.[49] In *Seven*, Eteocles worries that his name will be on every Theban's lips should the city fall (6). The implication is that the Thebans will curse him for failing to save the city.[50] He then prays that Zeus the Defender be true to his name and defend the city (9). This preoccupation with appropriate naming is something which recurs in *Seven*. Eteocles hopes that the symbol of Night on Tydeus' shield will be true to her name and bring the night of death on Tydeus' own eyes, turning the device against him (403-6). Conversely, it is remarked that Parthenopaeus' savagery does not correspond to his maidenish name, from *parthenos* 'virgin' (536), a sign that a name should not always be trusted.[51] Most notably, however, the meaning of 'Eteocles' as 'true-glory' in Greek (*eteon + kleos*), and of 'Polynices' as 'much-strife' (*polu + neikos*) is exploited throughout the play. Amphiaraus dwells on the significance of Polynices' name (576-8), and Eteocles claims that his brother is aptly named (658). In the same speech, Eteocles trusts that Justice would be utterly false to her name if she consorted with Polynices, and so goes to face Polynices himself (670-1). The Chorus later lament at 828-31 that the brothers died in manners true to their names.[52] Indeed, the outcome was homonymous for both the aptly named brothers, as they were both stricken on the 'well-named' (i.e. left-hand) side (888).

The stressed etymology of the brothers' names has affected scholarly interpretation of which brother is more at fault. Polynices is often branded the rogue in contrast to Eteocles. But in Chapter 2 it was argued that both brothers are presented as equally to blame, and one scholar has suggested an alternative etymology for 'Eteocles' as 'true-weeping' (from *eteon + klaiô*).[53] In any case the outcome seems to be described for both as 'of the same name', 'homonymous' (984).[54] Eteocles' hopes that the gods will be true to their names, and his statement that Polynices is true to his represents the same failure to grasp reality as did his reproaches of the Chorus' expressions of prayer. Just as he too was guilty of inauspicious speech, so he must also die along with Polynices if Justice and Zeus are to be true to their names.

Oracles, prophets, and dreams

Laius' consultation of the oracle of Apollo is something to which classical Greeks could relate. Seeking oracular advice was commonplace amongst Greeks and there were several oracular shrines throughout Greece, the best known being that of Apollo at Delphi and that of Zeus at Dodona. The Athenian assembly could seek guidance from an oracle on any number of topics, and we have several references to oracle consultations before military campaigns.[55] Herodotus tells us that advice was sought from Delphi by the Athenians before the Persian campaign (7.141-2). When they received a prophecy suggesting disaster, they approached the oracle a second time and begged Apollo for a more favourable oracle. A second oracle was duly pronounced, the famous prophecy that the wooden walls of Athens alone would hold firm, which turned out to be the 'walls' of the navy who dealt a crushing defeat on the Persians at Salamis.

It is interesting to note here that it does not seem to be unusual to ask for a different prophecy if the first is unsatisfactory. Thus, no blame can be attributed to Laius for returning to the oracle three times in an attempt to receive a different one. The fault comes when he disregards the prophecy in spite of having received the same oracle three times. As the Chorus in *Seven* note, 'oracles do not lose their edge' (844), and as the Theban saga demonstrates, no effort, however great, to avert the course of a divine oracle can prevail. In Sophocles' *Oedipus the King*, Jocasta and Laius had received an oracle that their son would grow up to kill his father and marry his mother. They order the infant to be exposed in the hope that his death will prevent the fulfilment of the oracle, but, as we know, Oedipus survives and lives to fulfil the dreaded prophecy.

Where travel to consult an oracle is not convenient, a more immediate source of divine insight is the prophet. Prophets were another real feature of Greek life. They practised divination through reading the signs of birds and by examining the entrails of sacrificial animals. Although in every day life, prophets could be viewed as charlatans, in poetry their divinations are never wrong.[56] In *Seven* there are two prophets who feature: Tiresias, the Theban prophet, and Amphiaraus, prophet among the attackers. There is little mention of Tiresias in *Seven*, indeed his identity is implied rather than specified. He is simply called 'the prophet' at 24. He is blind but has an 'infallible skill' at reading bird signs and is 'the master of this kind of prophecy' (26-7). He declares that an attack against Thebes is being prepared and Eteocles is wise to believe him.

Amphiaraus' prophetic foresight is unfortunately no boon to him. Bound as he is by oath to take part in the expedition, discussed further in Chapter 4, he marches knowingly to his own doom. Both the Scout and Eteocles acknowledge and revere his divine powers, and he is the only one of the attackers who is not impious or arrogant in some way. Amphiaraus is reported as exclaiming that he will enrich the land of Thebes by becoming a prophet buried in its soil (587-9). This will have struck a chord with original spectators familiar with the oracular shrine of Amphiaraus near Thebes. The words of Amphiaraus thus convey the aetiology (or mythological explanation) behind the foundation of this contemporary oracular shrine, something which tragedy frequently does.[57]

Connected to the realm of prophecy is that of dreams. In one version of the divine struggle for possession of the Delphic oracle, it is explained why mortals misinterpret dreams although their symbolism is true. When Apollo, as a child, forcibly took the seat from Earth's daughter Themis, she retaliated by sending mortals prophetic dreams, making Apollo's oracle redundant. Apollo then appealed to his father Zeus for help, and Zeus deprived mortals of the ability to interpret their dreams, thus restoring the importance of the Delphic oracle (Euripides, *Iphigenia among the Taurians*, 1234-82). Dreams are an important motif in much of classical Greek literature, and the plays of Aeschylus are no exception. All his extant plays contain some engagement with dreams.[58]

In *Seven*, we are clearly missing some background information which would have been provided in the previous play(s). On the point of going to meet his brother, Eteocles states 'it was too true what I saw in those dream-visions about the dividing of our father's property' (710-11). This suggests a misinterpreted dream based on the ambiguous curse of Oedipus that the brothers would be reconciled by a Scythian stranger. Eteocles and the Chorus have now realized that the 'stranger' is 'cruel-hearted Iron' (727-33), and it has been suggested that the Chorus may be interpreting the lost dream in their third choral song (second stasimon).[59]

Divine causation

We saw in Chapter 2 how the two brothers each bear some responsibility for the fulfilment of the Curse but, as with other Aeschylean treatments of causation and responsibility, human decisions and divine design both play their part. There are clearly human errors made which precipitate the chain of events, but the gods are also presented as responsible for the final outcome. We have seen how the Curse, the *daimôn*, and Ares are prominent players in the orchestration of doom, and Apollo is also responsible. He is presented as wreaking the consequences of Laius' act of foolishness on the offspring of Oedipus (801-2). What does this mean? If the gods have predetermined the fate of the house of Thebes, do human actions matter? The answer has to be 'yes'. Laius was clearly told the dire consequences of his producing offspring and yet he chose to ignore these, an action which amounts to madness. But the actions of Polynices and Eteocles also matter. Polynices *decides* to march on Thebes, and Eteocles *decides* to station himself against his brother. Are these actions divinely inspired? Probably, but this is not the only motivating factor in human decisions. By the time Eteocles posts himself to the seventh gate, he seems to have become the agent of the Curse. But the fact remains that by sending out all the other defending champions first, he leaves himself little option but to meet his brother.

It is curious too that the Curse is twice referred to as 'swift' in the play (744, 791). This seems quite inappropriate. The fulfilment of the Curse on Laius (his death and Oedipus' marriage to Jocasta) happens years after the birth of Oedipus, when he has reached adulthood. Similarly the Curse on Oedipus is only revealed to him after he has fathered children with Jocasta. We do not know exactly how long has passed in *Seven* since Oedipus cursed his sons, but it is a matter of years rather than months – enough time for Oedipus to have died, for Eteocles to have reigned longer than he should, and for Polynices to have married and gathered an army. However, if we infer that the Curse is 'swift' once human action has been taken to set it in motion, the concept of the Curse as 'swift' becomes far more intelligible. The Curse on Laius is fulfilled by his leaving Thebes when Oedipus leaves Corinth, allowing their paths to cross. Oedipus' search for the murderer of Laius is what precipitates his discovery of the Curse in Sophocles, at least. And here in *Seven* it is Polynices marching on Thebes and Eteocles posting himself to the seventh gate which accomplish the fulfilment of the Curse. We must conclude that it is a combination of both divine and human agency which causes the Curse to manifest itself.[60]

4

Warriors

As a genre developed and inspired by its literary predecessors of epic and lyric poetry, Greek tragedy was inevitably concerned with portraying the warriors and heroes which featured so strongly in earlier poetry and were staples of Greek myth. We know from extant plays and fragments that the Theban saga was a particularly popular subject for tragedy, and the influence of *Seven* on later tragedy will be discussed in Chapter 6. Of all the Theban tragedies, however, *Seven* is the most concerned with heroic warriors and warfare of a type familiar from epic. This chapter will examine the conduct of the warriors in *Seven* both in terms of heroic ideology, focusing on the shield scene, where the symbols on each shield represent an attempt by the warrior to control his fate, and in the context of fifth-century prejudices against barbarians.

Heroic identity

The focus in *Seven* is very much on the individual leaders of the expedition with little mention of their supporting armies. The military prowess of individual warriors is stressed in a manner familiar from the *Iliad*, and the war at Thebes is effectively decided by a series of single-combat duels, a form of warfare which is, again, very much a preoccupation of the *Iliad*. It is noteworthy that fifth-century accounts of the Persian wars, in which Aeschylus had fought, focus on the military superiority of the Greeks as a whole, not on that of individual heroes.[1] This context very much presents the world of *Seven* as a past age of heroes for a contemporary audience.

This is a world of princes, all of whom are inevitably excellent warriors, bound on a campaign of war with complete annihilation of the enemy as their ultimate goal. Because this is a world of princes, their armour is beautiful and intricately designed, proof of their material wealth. In *Seven*, as at several points in the *Iliad*, the shields of the warriors are especially important, as will be discussed below. The attackers ride into battle on chariots (*Seven* 151, 204), typically used in Homer (but not in classical hoplite warfare) to convey warriors with speed to a suitable point for dismounting before rushing into hand to hand combat on foot.[2]

The quarrel which causes the war in *Seven* may be compared to the cause of the Trojan expedition in that it originates in a private dispute in which the injured party gathers an army to attack the offender and retrieve what he deems to be his. Although there is a strong focus on individuals, the expedition is presented as a public venture where the attackers in *Seven* are, like the Greeks in the *Iliad*, seen collectively as Achaeans (28, 324) and Argives (59, 120, 679). In such heroic warfare there is no real concept of surrender. Once the Trojans in the *Iliad* have rejected the proposals of the Achaeans, each side seeks the total annihilation of the other.[3] In theory, this remained the goal of archaic and classical Greek warfare, though in practice compromises were often reached.[4] The prime motives for war in both *Seven* and the *Iliad* are vengeance, recovery of status, the opportunity to prove superiority over the enemy, and the possibility of gaining wealth and war plunder (cf. *Seven* 232, 335, 454, 479, 482).[5] All these motives are tied up in the values of heroic society, a shame-culture where honour and reputation are of essential importance for heroic identity and any affront on the honour of a hero or his community (such as the theft of a woman or the usurpation of power) must be avenged.[6] The greatest heroes are also the wealthiest and expect the best prizes. Achilles withdraws from fighting in the *Iliad* because Agamemnon has insulted his honour by confiscating his prize Briseis.[7] The kind of illegitimate arrogance displayed by Agamemnon in this incident, which leads to the dishonour of another hero, is an example of what the Greeks termed *hybris*.[8] The term is used twice in *Seven* (406, 502), in both cases by Eteocles to describe the arrogant confidence of the attackers, which he hopes will be their downfall.

Against the backdrop of Homeric epic we can trace the similarities in heroic ideology but we can also observe some unsettling differences. There are several passages in the *Iliad* which show that a warrior should be open to reconciliation even if this is not often achieved.[9] In *Iliad* 3, the Greeks and the Trojans swear to a general truce, with the war to be settled by single combat between Menelaus and Paris, but the truce is broken by the Trojan ally Pandarus under the influence of Athena, and war resumes. The saga of the war against Thebes also contains suggested terms for reconciliation in some versions. In Euripides' *Phoenician Women* (446-637), Polynices first enters Thebes under truce and offers terms which Eteocles rejects. Later they agree to decide the issue by single combat in which they both die (1217-1424). In *Seven* there are never any terms suggested for reconciliation and the meeting of the two brothers in single combat is not a joint decision intended to settle the affair and spare the lives of others. The decision in Euripides is 'most shameful rashness' (1219-20). Engaging kin in single combat goes against nature in a heroic context where enemies, like Glaucus and Diomedes, who discover that their fathers had been guest-friends, can exchange armour on the battlefield as a gesture of goodwill instead of engaging in combat (*Iliad* 6.199-236). Indeed, the pathos of the Theban fratricide was a popular motif in ancient funerary art, appearing on several Hellenistic funerary urns as well as on Roman sarcophagi. Presumably the image was chosen to emphasize an untimely or unnecessary death which was to be much lamented (Fig. 3).[10]

A further consideration is the mentality of the warriors and their attitudes to violence. The majority of recent scholars, who have dealt with the issue of heroic mentality, have generally disagreed with the thesis put forward by the classical

Fig. 3. Funerary urn, dating from the end of the first half of the second century BC; Archaeological Museum of Florence, Inv. N. 5713.

scholar Adkins, from 1960 onwards, that moral responsibility was relatively unimportant in Greek ethics.[11] Fighting with a view to total destruction of the enemy is in keeping with the mechanics of war and the responsibilities of the warriors but, as we saw in Chapter 3, several of the attacking warriors in *Seven* display a dangerous disregard for divine power which is certainly to be viewed as impious, if not immoral and irresponsible. The recklessness of the individual attackers in *Seven* goes against heroic practice in Homer, where self-preservation is the ultimate goal rather than self-sacrifice.[12] The contrast between the attitudes of the attacking warriors in Homer's *Iliad* and Aeschylus' *Seven* is perhaps best illustrated by the oath sacrifices described in each work. In the *Iliad*, we are shown an oath sacrifice accompanying a truce and marking a chance at peace, in *Seven* we are presented with a pre-battle oath sacrifice which marks the inevitability of war.[13]

The shield scene

The black shield used in the oath sacrifice (43) ties into a pattern of ominous references to 'black' in *Seven*, such as the black curse of Oedipus (695, 832) and the black Fury (977, 988).[14] The description of the attackers' shields as 'white' by the panicked Chorus (90) only serves to relate the information that the attackers are Argives, known in tragedy by the epithet 'of the white-shields'.[15] In fact, when the Scout returns from his reconnaissance mission, we hear in detail the exact description of each man's shield. Each of these descriptions is an *ekphrasis*, that is an extended and detailed literary description of an object. Furthermore, each *ekphrasis* is imbued with semiotic meaning, that is the signs and symbols on each shield are open to analysis. In each case the symbols are interpreted by Eteocles who also attempts to counteract their force. The shield scene has attracted much analysis from scholars and has been analysed from different theoretical perspectives: hermeneutic (a term used to describe the process of interpretation), where Eteocles' interpretations of the shield symbols are what is at issue;[16] semiotic, where the meanings of the shield symbols are the main concern;[17] and structuralist (a theory according to which identity can be created by defining oneself against an opposite 'Other'), where the shield-scene is read as 'a developmental model for self and society'.[18] The imagery of the shield scene has also been well discussed.[19]

Shield semiotics

The image on the shield of each attacker in *Seven* represents a particular threat to the city and acts as a representation of the character of its bearer. There is some historical evidence to suggest that armies did emboss their shields with symbols of their provenance in ancient Greece. How widespread this was in the early fifth century is uncertain; by the early fourth century the concept of swapping shields to fool the enemy could be successfully employed precisely because of such identifying symbols. Xenophon tells of how, during the Corinthian War, a Spartan commander Pasimachus was able to fool the Argive enemy by taking up the shields of their Sicyonian allies, distinguished by the Σ (sigma) on their shields (*Hellenica* 4.4.10). Similarly, Sparta had shields distinguished by the Λ (lambda) to signify Lakedaimôn, i.e. Spartan.[20] One story also survives of a Spartan with a life-size fly as a symbol on his shield, who responded to taunts about the image with the reply that he got close enough to his enemies for them to see the true size of his symbol (Plutarch, *Moralia* 234C-D.41).[21] In poetry, however, set in the time of the heroes, shield designs are far more elaborate and majestic, adorned with apotropaic images, and often subjects of ekphrastic treatment. The shield of Agamemnon in the *Iliad* is adorned with ten circles of bronze and twenty knobs of shining tin with another knob of dark cobalt in the centre, but 'circled in the midst of all was the blank-eyed face of the Gorgon with her dread stare, and round-about her were Fear and Terror' (11.32-7). The Gorgon also features on the shield of Lamachus in Aristophanes' *Acharnians*, terrorizing Dicaeopolis (574).

The shield of Heracles described in a work attributed to the poet Hesiod is exceptionally detailed and fearsome (*The Shield* 139-320). It features Fear with glowing eyes and frightening teeth, Strife hovering at his brow. Pursuit, Flight, Tumult, Panic, Slaughter, Uproar, and Fate, draped in the blood of men, are all present. There are twelve snakes, and droves of boars and lions depicted. Many mythological heroes and battles and several Olympian gods are all represented, as is the Darkness of Death with blood dripping from her cheeks. The presentation of this shield was certainly influenced by the description of the shield of Achilles in the *Iliad* (18.478-607),[22] perhaps the best known *ekphrasis* from ancient literature. But Achilles' shield is problematic. A feature of the shield which has often perplexed scholars is the strong presence of peacetime imagery. Hate, Confusion, and Death make a brief appearance (535) but there is a strong emphasis on agriculture, dancing, and peaceful city life. Oliver Taplin has argued that the symbolism on the shield reflects the broader structure of the *Iliad*, which, while its primary focus is grim warfare, is also concerned to keep the audience aware of the contrast with peacetime.[23] Indeed even the shield of Heracles, for all its grimness, is finished off with an extended description of prosperous city life, notably in a seven-gated city (*The Shield* 270-320). This is interesting in the context of seven-gated Thebes as it highlights the depth of utter darkness and disaster which pervades the Aeschylean play. In *Seven* there are no joyful dancing girls, just a panic-stricken and frenzied Chorus, and agricultural imagery is perverted into the metaphor of the field of the mother ploughed by the son (753-4). There is no reference to peaceful government. Instead the dispute over government and rights to property is the cause of the war. What all this reflects is the unnatural basis on which Thebes is built and the perverted nature of this fratricidal war. In *Seven* there are no references to a healthy state of Thebes even before the invading army attacks. Rather the play is relentless in its imagery of destruction and savagery.

First gate (Proetid Gate): Tydeus vs. Melanippus

Tydeus, first named of the attackers, is one of the most terrifying. He growls near the Proetid gate and shrieks like a snake hissing at midday (that time being ideally suited for snakes to hunt warm-blooded prey who take rest from the heat in the shade). He tosses the tall plumes of his helmet as he writhes with battle lust, a powerful image of a crazed aggressor hungry to attack its prey. Apart from the inhuman sounds coming from Tydeus himself, his shield is fitted with bells of beaten bronze which clang dramatically as he moves (385-6). This concentration of movement and noise contrasts with the silent symbol on his shield: a full moon surrounded by a blazing firmament full of stars. It may not be immediately apparent why this image should be threatening or, indeed, arrogant in the way that it is interpreted (387, 391, 404). The representation of Night on the shield is important, and ties in with the fact that the attackers are said to be operating under the shadow of night (29). Night is clearly a dangerous time. It shrouds ambushes and reconnaissance missions. Aeschylus elsewhere calls the Furies the daughters of Night (*Eumenides* 321-2, 416). This association works well with the image of Tydeus himself acting like a snake. But the moon and stars are themselves significant. They grant the ability to see in the dark, captured in the description of the full moon as being 'the eye of Night' (390), and in this image of the full moon lies Tydeus' potential arrogance. Tydeus presents himself as greatest among warriors in the same way as the full moon on his shield is said to be 'the greatest of the stars' (390). A fragment of lyric poetry from the early sixth century BC describes the effect of the full moon on its surroundings: 'The stars about the lovely moon | withdraw and hide their shining forms | when at her full she bathes the earth in light' (Sappho fragment 34, translated by M. West). The full moon causes the other stars, however bright, to fade in comparison, the implication being that Tydeus intends to overshadow even his companions in his arrogance.

Tydeus 'screams' again, and raves, this time like a 'horse panting against the force of bit and bridle who impatiently awaits the sound of the trumpet' (393-4). This time it is Tydeus' physical strength and determination which are stressed through the image of the horse. The bad omens which prevent Tydeus from crossing the river are forcefully checking his battle-mad spirit, leading him to hurl insults at Amphiaraus, the interpreter of the omens. Tydeus is traditionally small in stature (*Iliad* 5.801), but this feature of his appearance is suppressed in *Seven*. It may be implied by the fact that Capaneus is described as taller than Tydeus, but both are said to be giants (424-5), a reference not only to their size but also to their antagonistic relationship with the Olympian gods, since the giants were enemies of the gods. It remains that the figure of Tydeus is a terrifying assault on the senses. The three crests of his helmet which move with Tydeus' writhing and cast long shadows create a dramatic and awesome image. He has the chthonic qualities of an aggressive snake coupled with the imposing physical strength of a horse – a deadly combination. But although it is easy to visualize Tydeus through the Scout's description, it is perhaps the aural dimension to the character which has the most impact. He growls, screams, hisses, shouts insults, clangs forth the bells on his shield, and pants in anticipation of another sound – the trumpet call to battle.

'Who can be relied on to stand before Proetus' Gate when its bolts are undrawn?' asks the Scout (395-6). We imagine the force of Tydeus bursting through the gate at the very moment of unbolting, so eager is he for the battle. Tydeus, as the first attacker, forms a counterpart to Polynices, the last, in that they are both sons-in-law of Adrastus and had both urged him to support them in restoring them to their rightful throne. Both are blamed for the expedition by Amphiaraus (570ff.). Tydeus has a vested interest in the success of the mission, more than simply material gain from sacking Thebes. Once Polynices has been reinstated at Thebes, it will be his turn to regain his rightful kingdom with the support of Adrastus. What Tydeus stands to gain from sacking Thebes thus makes him an even more formidable and determined enemy.

Interestingly, Eteocles appears unfazed and picks up on the crucial elements left unmentioned in the description of Tydeus: his weapons rather than his armour. Shield-devices cannot inflict wounds, nor can crests or bells hurt without a spear (400). Of course Tydeus must have a spear, but this aspect of his armour has not been specified. With regard to the shield symbol, Eteocles is able to turn it against the attacker. Perhaps the most common expression for death in Greek poetry is 'to no longer see the light'. Eteocles uses this to suggest that Tydeus' shield symbol will be a prophecy against himself, with the night of death falling on his own eyes. Against him, Eteocles chooses Melanippus as champion for two main reasons: he hates arrogance and is tied to the land of Thebes as one of the Sown men whom Ares spared. Melanippus is said to honour the throne of Modesty (409), suggesting that he will have the divine favour of this deity against the arrogant Tydeus, and although Ares is unpredictable in his dealings, it is possible, at least, that he will favour Melanippus also. In any case, Melanippus' dedication to the land of Thebes makes it clear that he will fight to the death to defend her as his 'mother'.

Second gate (Electran Gate): Capaneus vs. Polyphontes

Capaneus is a giant greater still than Tydeus and his boasts against Zeus and the gods are said to show 'a pride beyond human limits' (425). On his shield he has 'a naked man carrying fire' and 'the torch with which he is armed blazes in his hands, and in golden letters he declares "I will burn this city" ' (432-4). In contrast to the cacophonous presence of Tydeus, the only 'sound' which comes from Capaneus is a paradoxical 'silent declaration': the voice of the inscription on his shield. This is an intriguing feature of references to writing in Greek tragedy. The silent written word is often presented as a personified voice, the best-known example being the suicide letter of Phaedra in Euripides' *Hippolytus* which shouts forth at 877-80. In *Seven*, however, each of the three inscribed shields, of which Capaneus' is the first, combines text and image so that the figure on the shield is to be imagined as speaking the words inscribed.

The description of Capaneus is far less detailed than that of Tydeus. The initial impact has been made by the terrifying figure of Tydeus, but Capaneus represents a different threat. He rejects the thunderbolts of Zeus in favour of human fire. There is no armour described apart from the shield itself whose symbol represents Capaneus' only weapon – fire. The threat of destruction by fire would surely have struck a chord with an Athenian audience who had recently endured the ravages of fire at the hands of the Persians during their siege of Athens in 480.[24] Even the Scout fails to see how such a threat can be met. He breaks off mid-sentence at 435: 'Against such a man you must send – but who can stand against him?' But Eteocles dismisses Capaneus with great ease. His boasts will be his downfall, the fire of Zeus (i.e. the thunderbolt) will seek him out, and a reliable defender of fiery spirit,

Polyphontes, has already been posted against him 'with the goodwill of Artemis the Protectress and the aid of the other gods' (449-50). Eteocles is so confident that Capaneus will be easily dispatched that he ends his speech by urging the Scout to reveal the next attacking champion. In mythological terms, Eteocles is entirely correct to feel that Capaneus will fall. As the audience knows, his boasts against Zeus come back to haunt him and he is killed by Zeus' thunderbolt. The image of early man carrying fire might also bring to mind the figure of Prometheus who stole fire from the gods to give it to humans and received terrible punishment from Zeus as a consequence (dramatized in *Prometheus Bound*).

Third gate (Neïstan Gate) Eteoclus vs. Megareus

Although he has a name which differs from that of Eteocles in just one letter, Eteoclus is the attacker who is most strongly presented as barbarian, as discussed below. Like Tydeus, the figure of Eteoclus is full of motion. He circles with his horses 'who are snorting in their harness, eager to fall on the gate' (461-2). Eteoclus' shield too bears a threat in its adornment. A fully armed warrior scales the city walls with a ladder intending to sack the city. This figure also speaks; it 'cries out in written syllables saying that not even Ares can throw him off the wall' (466-9). The emphasis here is on the attacker's equipment. He is well armed and has successfully mounted a scaling ladder to the enemy walls. But, again, this is combined with a boast, this time in defiance of Ares. An appropriate defender has already been dispatched: Megareus, another of the descendants of the Sown men. It is particularly appropriate that Megareus has this connection with Ares in going to face the attacker who defies this god. He is also a man who 'bears his boast in his hands' (473), that is, he is a figure of action rather than words. But Eteocles is not sure whether Megareus will prevail (477-9), once again highlighting the arbitrary nature of Ares as a god. If Megareus fails, he will certainly die in defence of the land which nourished him (477).

Fourth gate (Gate of Athena Onca): Hippomedon vs. Hyperbius

As the first figure in the second triad of attackers, Hippomedon corresponds to Tydeus in being particularly terrifying. This is evidenced by the fact that the Scout admits to shuddering at the sight of Hippomedon (490). He is a vast figure. The metaphor of the 'great round threshing-floor of a shield' which he brandishes is testimony to his huge stature. If the shield is the size of a threshing-floor, then the man who bears it must be of equivalent size. As with the shield of Tydeus, the emblem on the intricately wrought shield of Hippomedon corresponds to primeval time. On the shield is depicted the monster Typhon with his hundred snake heads. He emits 'dark smoke ... from his fire-breathing lips' and snakes coil round the circle of the 'hollow-bellied shield' (493-6). This monster was the last opponent Zeus conquered before taking control of the universe (Hesiod *Theogony* 853-68). Like Tydeus, Hippomedon is loud and raging for battle. He is said to utter loud cries and to be raising a great war-cry (487, 497). As we noted in Chapter 3, he is possessed by Ares, and the Scout sees him as the personification of Terror himself (500). But more interesting perhaps is the suggestion that 'he rages for a fight like a maenad, with a fearsome look in his eye' (498). A maenad was a female follower of Dionysus possessed by the god and liable to act in a wild and savage manner. The best-known example of maenadic savagery comes from Euripides' *Bacchae*, in a much earlier part of the Theban saga involving the family of its founder Cadmus (his daughter Agave and her son Pentheus, then king). There the god Dionysus punishes Thebes for neglecting his worship by driving all the women of Thebes into a maenadic frenzy. The women go hunting wild beasts in the mountains, and in her maenadic trance the king's mother Agave ends up tearing what she thinks is a lion limb from limb. She comes back with its head fixed on a stake, a symbol of victory, but as she regains consciousness, she realizes to her horror that it is her own son she has killed so savagely.

It is unusual for a male warrior to be compared to a maenad.

If a comparison to a savage beast is required the lion serves the purpose most appropriately. Indeed comparison to a lion is one of the most frequent similes to describe a warrior in the *Iliad*. In the description of Hippomedon, there is no doubt that he is an alpha male warrior and the comparison to a maenad does not necessarily detract from this. That he 'rages for a fight like a maenad' is combined with the statement that he is possessed by Ares. What is emphasized therefore is the notion of possession. Hippomedon is possessed not only by the spirit of war but also by the spirit of savage dismemberment, the Dionysiac *sparagmos*. Both forces are divinely inspired and this is what makes the maenad simile more effective than a comparison to a lion. It is not that Hippomedon's aggression is *like* that of a savage beast, it is that he is possessed by savagery itself, and this force manifests itself in the 'fearsome look in his eye'. The look in the eye, of course, is an indication of possession or disturbance, recognized in antiquity as it is today. Both Ares and Athena, as war deities, have a terrifying gaze,[25] and in poetic descriptions of divinely induced madness distorted vision is a common feature.[26]

Eteocles' first response is to evoke the allegiance of Athena Onca, guardian of the fourth gate, who 'protects her nestlings from a hostile serpent' (503). That Athena is known to wear the aegis – the pectoral displaying Medusa's head given to her by Perseus – shows that she has no time for primeval snake monsters such as Typhon. Indeed it is at this gate that the description of the defender bodes best and induces most confidence, even after the grim figure of Hippomedon has been fleshed out. Where Hippomedon's weapons remain unmentioned, Hyperbius is said to be 'faultless in form, in spirit, and also in the handling of arms' (507-8), and he is the only defender whose shield is described and used as a direct counterweight to the shield emblem of the attacker. On Hyperbius' shield sits 'Father Zeus, standing with his flaming thunderbolt in his hand' (512-13). As Eteocles points out, the attackers are thus on the side of the losers, the Thebans on the side of the winners, if, by extension of the images on their shields, theogonic history repeats itself and Zeus quashes Typhon. The reference to Zeus as 'Father' is important too as it refers to his role as ruler of the universe established only *after* having subdued Typhon, therefore anticipating that the same symbolic victory will be achieved at the fourth gate. Zeus would thus become Hyperbius' 'saviour', Eteocles says, referring to another of Zeus' commonest epithets.

The impetus behind these statements is the desire for Zeus to be true to his name, an issue which was discussed in Chapter 3. The fact that Zeus' thunderbolt is 'flaming' demonstrates a more powerful weapon of attack since Typhon's fire-breathing lips are said to let out only 'dark smoke'. The smoke is clearly meant to indicate that fire lies beneath it – Typhon is like a fire-breathing dragon figure, who emits smoke between breaths of fire. But smoke can be an ambiguous symbol where fire is concerned. Much smoke can indicate a weak fire in its infancy, before its blaze catches on. The smoke on Hippomedon's shield is described as the 'sister of flame' reinforcing this distinction between smoke and fire. Typhon's primeval fire is weak in comparison to the new fire of Zeus' thunderbolt.

Fifth gate (North Gate): Parthenopaeus vs. Actor

At the fifth gate stands a young warrior, 'little more than a boy', but whose 'savage pride' is 'not at all in keeping with his maidenish name' (533-6): Parthenopaeus (whose name and its meaning was discussed in Chapter 3 and n. 51). The reference to Hippomedon as 'like a maenad' in the Scout's previous speech may partly have been to prepare us for this girlish man who must nevertheless be feared. If a raging warrior like Hippomedon can be compared to a female figure, it is easier to believe that Parthenopaeus, whose cheeks are just getting thick with down (534), can be taken seriously as a warrior. Like Hippomedon, Parthenopaeus also has a fierce look in his eye, a gorgon's stare (537). It is part of his blasphemy that he values his spear above the gods and above 'his eyes' (i.e. his life). Interestingly, he is the only attacker whose weapon is mentioned along with his shield, bolstering his image as aggressor. Notably too, Parthenopaeus' name is suppressed throughout the description of the fifth attacker and is only revealed at the end of the Scout's speech. Again this heightens the impact of the figure as a threat to the city.

His shield bears a particularly insulting symbol for Thebes, 'the city's disgrace', the Sphinx (539-41). The Sphinx, as we know, had plagued Thebes during the reign of Laius, devouring its inhabitants (hence she is the 'eater of raw flesh' at 541), until Oedipus had arrived and solved her riddle. The insult to Thebes is the reminder of how many of its citizens were destroyed by the Sphinx, but we may wonder how dangerous this symbol really is for the city. Like Typhon, the Sphinx is a monster which has already been defeated. She is an enemy of Thebes, to be sure, but she has already lost against the Cadmeans. However, there is a detail of the image which heightens its danger to Thebes. Under her, the Sphinx 'bears a man, one of the Cadmeans – so that many weapons may be thrown at that man' (543-4). The point is that in attacking Parthenopaeus, the Thebans risk hitting the Cadmean depicted on his shield, an unlucky omen for them. So the image is a more complex threat than it first appears.

Eteocles' reply this time begins with a general curse against all the attackers, breaking the pattern of responding directly to the threat of each warrior: 'May they obtain from the gods a fate that matches their own intentions, they and those unholy boasts of theirs; then they would surely perish utterly and wretchedly' (550-3). This highlights the particular insult of Parthenopaeus' shield which riles Eteocles, but also marks the culminations of boasts and blasphemies on the part of the attackers, with that of Parthenopaeus as one of the most extreme. It prepares us for a change of tack with Amphiaraus at the next gate, the true prophet and antithesis of boaster or blasphemer.

After this generalization, Eteocles turns his attention to providing an appropriate defender against Parthenopaeus. As in the contrast between Eteoclus and Megareus, Eteocles stresses action as opposed to speech. Actor is a man 'who does not boast but whose hand can see what needs to be done' (554). 'He will not allow a tongue with no deeds to its credit to flood through the gates and breed trouble' (555-6). It is an easy claim to make that someone as young as Parthenopaeus has no great deeds to his name, something which could not easily be said of the other champions. An important line of defence here too is not to allow the Sphinx into the city walls since this would be a bad omen for Thebes.

Sixth gate (Homoloïd Gate): Amphiaraus vs. Lasthenes

Amphiaraus is a threat unlike all other attackers. Eteocles has used their boasts and threats and shield symbols to turn their power against them. The blasphemers will be punished by the gods, the attacking powers associated with each symbol will be met with an opposing and, it is hoped, more powerful force. But Amphiaraus utters no threats or boasts against Thebes. The only ones he reviles are Tydeus and Polynices whom he sees as having instigated the expedition in which he was forced to take part. He abuses Tydeus first, but in mythological terms Polynices bears more responsibility for Amphiaraus' obligation to march on Thebes. Amphiaraus' wife Eriphyle was the sister of Adrastus, king of Argos. After a quarrel with his brother-in-law, Amphiaraus had sworn an oath that Eriphyle could decide the outcome on his behalf in any future dispute. When he refused to join the expedition against Thebes (knowing it to be doomed), Polynices (by now son-in-law to Adrastus) bribed Eriphyle with a Theban heirloom – the necklace of Harmonia – and she held Amphiaraus true to his oath, deciding that he should accompany the expedition.[27]

Far from being a blight on Thebes, Amphiaraus will be a benefit to the city giving rise to an oracular shrine through his death on Theban soil. He expects to die, but to die honourably, and his shield is completely blank because he does not wish to seem the bravest but to be the bravest (592). Amphiaraus knows he will die, but he is not going to die without a fight. So he represents a very particular threat. He is a brave and fearsome warrior and there is no blasphemy or shield symbol for Eteocles to counteract. Amphiaraus has accepted his fate and wields his shield calmly (590-1). The Scout recognizes that he is a danger precisely because he reveres the gods (595-6). It will take not only bravery but skill to defeat this man.

Eteocles' response is appropriate to the virtue of Amphiaraus whom he lauds as great prophet and pious man (610-11). An anecdote from Plutarch, writing in the second century AD, suggests that praise of Amphiaraus (especially lines 592-4) caused the original audience to turn their gaze to Aristides 'the Just' (a politician in fifth-century Athens), as if it were in praise of him. But the emphasis in the Aeschylean passage is not on 'justice', as the passage in Plutarch misquotes, but on 'excellence' or 'bravery' (*aristeia*) and the story, from an author writing several centuries after the play's first production, is undoubtedly fictional.[28] However, it is noteworthy that Amphiaraus is presented in such a positive light by Aeschylus, since in alternative traditions Amphiaraus fled from Thebes and was only spared the shame of being speared in the back by the intervention of the gods, who made the earth open to swallow him before he was hit (Pindar, *Nemean* 9.24-7). There were also versions in which Amphiaraus had been involved in the exiling of Adrastus and a betrayal of Tydeus.[29]

Against Amphiaraus is posted a man with several notable qualities. 'Powerful' Lasthenes is said to be 'a gatekeeper' who is 'stranger-hating' (621). This combines the notion that Amphiaraus will be kept out of the city, while at the same time aligning Lasthenes with the attackers whom Amphiaraus detests. They too were described as 'stranger-hating' a few lines earlier (606). This sets Lasthenes up as a reasonable antagonist for the faultless Amphiaraus. Lasthenes will attack Amphiaraus the foreigner rather than Amphiaraus the pious prophet. That Lasthenes will be the attacker at this gate rather than the defender is suggested by Eteocles who doubts whether Amphiaraus will attack the gate at all, not because he is lacking in spirit but because he has accepted his fate (615-18).

It is important too that Lasthenes is said to have 'a mature mind but youthful flesh' and 'a swift eye' (622-3). This gives him a mind with the potential to match that of the wise and experienced Amphiaraus but a superior physical strength and agility as the younger man. The suggestion that Lasthenes is 'not slow to seize with his spear on a spot exposed by a movement of the shield' (623-4) implies that Amphiaraus' death will be swift. It also anticipates that Amphiaraus will be skilled at defending himself in battle and that he will fall only because of Lasthenes' superior speed in attacking an area briefly exposed by shield movement. Even this kind of good fortune is said to be 'the gift of god' (625), showing that Lasthenes will conquer Amphiaraus only with the gods' will on his side. The cumulative effect of all this is a dexterous presentation of a skilled opponent, who, although he is fated to die, can only be overcome by a nimble warrior with a gift of good fortune from the gods. Amphiaraus' prowess as a warrior is confirmed also by the repeated formula 'the force of' repeated four times in this pair of speeches and used to describe Tydeus (571), Polynices (577), Amphiaraus (569), and Lasthenes (620). All are equally formidable warriors.

Seventh gate: Polynices vs. Eteocles

The seventh attacker is first described to Eteocles simply as 'your own brother' (632). His name is suppressed until later in the narrative, emphasizing the kinship between the two. His shield is, first of all, new (642). It is no ancestral piece of armour but a shield specially designed for this expedition. It is the most complex and detailed of all the shields, displaying two figures and a lengthy inscription: 'one beholds a man-at-arms, made of gold, led by a woman who walks ahead of him with modest gait. And as the writing proclaims, she says that she is Justice, "and I will bring this man back from exile, and he will possess his father's city and the right to dwell in his home" ' (643-8). The claim made by this shield is no timid one. Not only is Polynices coming back to take the throne of Thebes, but Justice herself is shown to lead him, giving a detailed message of her intention. Of course, as with all the shields, this is a man-made device, and the symbol on it represents the bearer's attempt to control his fate by associating himself with a particular power.

For an Athenian audience the shield of Polynices may have called to mind the return of the exiled sixth-century tyrant Pisistratus to Athens. We are told of a ruse concocted by Pisistratus and his future father-in-law Megacles after Pisistratus had been driven out of Athens. They find a young woman over six feet tall and dress her up in full armour, sending rumours around that the goddess Athena herself is leading Pisistratus back to Athens. The young woman then poses as Athena leading Pisistratus back to power (Herodotus, *Histories* 1.60). It is difficult to know what effect this parallel might have had on the audience. Athens had prospered under the rule of Pisistratus, which suggests that the parallel may have evoked sympathy for Polynices. On the other hand, the alleged patronage of the goddess had been a complete sham, and a rare example of Athenian witlessness, according to Herodotus.

With each attacker, Eteocles has found a matching defender with qualities appropriate to meeting his particular antagonist. Now he rejects the notion that Justice stands beside Polynices. He reminds us of 'the darkness of the womb' (664) which gave birth to Polynices, implying that Justice would never abide by the product of an incestuous union. Surely now, when he attacks his own fatherland, Justice will not be close by (666-7). Eteocles trusts that the Justice depicted on Polynices' shield is false, but, in contrast to his previous responses, he spends surprisingly little time defending himself as an appropriate match for his brother. There is, of course, a fundamental reason why Eteocles is *not* an appropriate opponent: this will inevitably lead to kindred bloodshed and pollution. But in one short sentence, which reminds us of this danger, Eteocles seems at pains to show that they are equally matched: he will go against Polynices as 'ruler against ruler, brother against brother, enemy against enemy' (674-5). The choral responses to

Eteocles' decision, discussed in Chapter 5, also emphasize a
state of madness or delusion which matches his brother's. The
point that they are equally matched foreshadows their mutual
slaughter. In the case of the first six attackers, an attempt had
been made to show that the defender was in some way *superior*
to the champion against whom he was posted. With the two
brothers, there is no superiority. As we saw in Chapter 2, they
must either both live, or both die.

The shield scene in perspective

There are several features of the shield scene which are more
easily appreciated through a retrospective overview. The collective identity of the Argives is stressed through emphasis on
their circular shields (489, 496, 540, 590, 591, 643), typical of
Argive warriors, and their use of horses (61, 206, 461, 475; cf.
392). Argos is known for its horses in Greek literature, called by
the epithet 'horse-pasturing' in Homer.[30] An obvious point is
that none of the attackers associates himself with an Olympian
power. Most align themselves with a primeval power, Eteoclus
trusts in human power, and Polynices trusts in the daughter of
Zeus (Justice). This foreshadows their doom against the
Thebans whose strong association with the more powerful
Olympian gods is evident through the presence of their statues
on the stage which represents Thebes, as discussed in Chapter
1. Also noteworthy is the development in the intricacy of the
shield designs as the scene progresses. Full moon and stars are
followed by a naked fire-bearer plus a two-word inscription,
followed in turn by an armed man scaling a city wall plus a
significantly longer inscription. Next we have a single monster,
but a complex, multi-headed one, emitting multi-coloured
smoke, and featuring snakes coiled all around the shield. Then
comes the composite Sphinx monster: human head and lion's
body with wings; and she holds a man beneath her. There is
obviously a break in the scheme with the blank shield of
Amphiaraus, but it picks up again with that of Polynices which
bears 'a double device' (643): two figures, one human, one

divine, one male, one female. The name of the female is inscribed on the shield, as are her words in the lengthiest of all the shield inscriptions.

The combination of image and text on three of the shields is interesting.[31] Aeschylus uses the metaphor of writing as memory elsewhere (*Suppliant Women* 179, 991; *Libation Bearers* 450-1; cf. *Prometheus Bound* 789), but the writing on the shields in *Seven* is striking. No other poetic shields are specifically inscribed with words in this way. It was stressed that the shield of Polynices is 'new' (642), but there is no doubt that *all* the shields were in fact designed (by Aeschylus) specifically for the assault on Thebes. Nowhere else, for example, would the figure of the Sphinx carrying a Theban be such a threatening insult to the citizens. Similarly, each of the three inscribed shields contains a direct message for the Thebans. Like the shield depictions themselves, these messages increase in complexity. The first 'I'll burn the city' is hardly necessary given the image of the fire-bearer which accompanies it. The message is quite clear even from the image alone. But the second inscription contains a message which cannot be discerned from the image itself: the defiance of Ares. The intention of succeeding in scaling the city walls is evident, but the inscribed message adds an extra dimension to the image with the words 'Not even Ares will throw me off these walls'. The image on Polynices' shield, however, is actually difficult to interpret without the inscription. It shows an armed warrior in gold with a woman leading him but it is only the writing which names the woman as Justice, and explains that she is bringing the man back from exile to regain possession of his father's house.

Sophisticated armour is always an indication of a prosperous and technologically advanced society in Greek poetry, but the introduction of inscribed messages on the shields is something new here, and the representation of literacy is a recurring motif in Greek tragedy throughout the fifth century. This reflects the excitement felt in fifth-century Athens about the rise of literate culture, though this was mixed with apprehension, and, more often than not, oral communication in tragedy is shown to be more reliable than written. Here too in *Seven*, we see that the written messages fail to come true, but the reference to writing which the Scout must be able to read is an interesting anachronism inserted into the oral culture of the heroic past.[32]

There are two other recurrent motifs in the shield scene: imagery of eyes and fire used to characterize the warriors. These both represent power and determination to destroy. The power which resides in the eyes was widely acknowledged by ancient Greeks. It was only by looking into the eyes of Medusa that victims were turned to stone, which is why the Gorgon was such a popular apotropaic image.[33] In theological terms a god could also be thought of as manifesting its presence through the eyes of its votive statue (as in Euripides' *Iphigenia among the Taurians*, 1167). Even the gagged Iphigenia can strike each of her sacrificers with an 'arrow' from her eye, a silent attack on those taking her life (*Agamemnon* 240-1). In Greek symposium culture also, eyes were an important image which often decorated the outside of drinking cups. As the cup was raised for drinking, the eyes of the drinker would become obscured and replaced by the large painted eyes of the cup, thus protecting the drinker from any evil stare.[34] Occasionally, the pupil of the eye was replaced by the face of the Gorgon.[35] The apotropaic eye is also found on images of ships in Greek art. In battle, the eyes of a warrior should inspire fear as much as his stature. When Hector is raging fiercely, he is said to have the eyes of the Gorgon (*Iliad* 8.349).

Among the attackers, it has been suggested that the typically circular Argive shields 'should be understood as indications of their affinity with eyes'.[36] But there is far more explicit eye imagery developed in the shield scene. In the case of Tydeus, the images of eyes and fire are directly connected. The metaphor of 'the eye of Night' on his shield is itself 'brilliant' in a 'blazing firmament' of stars (389-90). Capaneus associates himself with human fire, dismissing the divine fire of Zeus, a fatal error. Against him is posted Polyphontes, a man of 'fiery spirit' (448). The flaming thunderbolt of Zeus reappears at the fourth gate pitted against Typhon's 'fire-breathing lips' (493). Zeus is poised to hurl his bolt of fire while Typhon emits only smoke, a clear indication that the fire of Zeus will prevail. Nevertheless, Hippomedon will be a tough opponent, possessed as he is by Ares with a divinely inspired grim look in his eye (498). This possession by Ares is something captured in the recent pen and ink drawing by Aaron Ryan 'The Light of Ares', where the eyes of Hippomedon and Tydeus, identifiable by their shield symbols, glow with red undertones against a fiery red sky (Fig. 4, unfortunately reproduced here only in black and white).

Fig. 4. 'The Light of Ares', 2006. © Aaron Ryan.

With Parthenopaeus the eye imagery works in two ways. He has the most fearsome eyes of all, those of the Gorgon (537), but he has also rejected his vision and his life by valuing his spear above all else, including his own eyes (530). That the eyes are a metaphor for life shows that Parthenopaeus is doomed. Of the defenders, only one is described in terms of his eyes: Lasthenes.

Against Amphiaraus it is said he has 'a swift eye' (623), enabling him to spot a weak point at which to strike. The image here is one of dexterity rather than brute force, and this is appropriate in the context of Amphiaraus. His piety means he does not deserve a grim opponent.

The image of fire is exploited in different ways for the attackers and defenders. The Thebans are either metaphorically 'fiery' like Polyphontes, emphasizing their determination, or else aligned with the fire of Zeus, calling divine power to their side. The fire of the attackers, by contrast, is a far more negative image, associated with savage destruction. This makes sense in the circumstances: the attackers want to lay waste to the city and burn it thoroughly; the defenders want to dissociate themselves from such aggressive and rampant fire. But there is a sense in which the brothers are destroyed by fire nonetheless, since fire is the element used to create the iron which enables their mutual slaughter, as referred to at 943-4. The image of iron itself is exclusively negative in this play. The attackers are said to have an 'iron-minded spirit' when they take their grim oath (52). Iron is also 'savage-minded' and 'harsh' (730; cf. 941). Of course, iron is the 'Scythian stranger' which will apportion the brothers their due, but connection with Scythia also emphasizes savagery. Inhabiting the area roughly equivalent to the modern-day Balkans, Scythian tribes were known for their gruesome customs including human sacrifice and cannibalism (Herodotus, *Histories* 4.103, 106). One tribe, the Neuri, were said to be werewolves (Herodotus, *Histories* 4.105). In general, among the Scythians, Ares receives a particular cult worship (Herodotus, *Histories* 4.60-3). In war, Scythians were said to be brutal enemies, practising decapitation and scalping, making drinking-cups out of enemy skulls and cloaks out of enemy skins. They also drink the blood of their enemies (Herodotus, *Histories* 4.64-6). The detail that the iron is Scythian in *Seven* (728, 817) thus consolidates the image of the gruesome slaughter it causes.

The contrast between the (empty) words of the attackers and the actions of the defenders is crystallized through the imagery of hands, associated exclusively with the defenders. For Megareus, his hands are his boast (473), Actor's hand sees what needs to be done (554), and Lasthenes' hand is swift (623). Even the hand of Zeus is on the defenders' side (513).[37] This image of hands is pitted against the empty boasts of the attackers, creating a contrast quite common in Greek tragedy, the opposition between speech and action.[38] So Eteocles stresses Theban action against the blustery boasts of the attackers, but a distinct irony of the shield scene is that several of the statements which Eteocles applies to the attackers could equally well be applied to him, though he will remain completely oblivious to this. He dismisses the symbol on Tydeus' shield with the words 'perhaps someone's folly may become prophetic' (402). He means that Tydeus has been foolish to choose Night as his symbol, but it also foreshadows Eteocles' own folly in going to meet his brother which proves to be the ultimate fulfilment of Apollo's prophecy. In this context, the irony of Eteocles' response to Capaneus is even more pointed. 'Men's foolish pride, you see, finds a truthful accuser in their own tongues' (439-40). As the Chorus will suggest, by deciding to face Polynices, Eteocles becomes like the brother he reviles (677-8).

The attackers as barbarians

The conscious delineation of a contrast between 'Greek' and 'barbarian' is a feature of many Greek tragedies.[39] The impetus for this dichotomy, which does not exist in the same way in archaic poetry, is generally understood as having been triggered by (the ultimately unsuccessful) Persian attacks on Greece in the first quarter of the fifth century. It was a matter of great pride for the Greeks, especially the Athenians, that they had decisively driven off an enemy of vastly superior numbers in a series of dramatic battles. Aeschylus, as an Athenian citizen, had fought against the Persians at the Battle of Marathon in 490 BC (for which, as we noted in Chapter 2, he was remembered on his epitaph), and he may have fought at the Battle of Salamis in 480 BC. The latter, a naval battle, is the subject of our earliest extant tragedy, by Aeschylus, *The Persians* (produced in 472 BC). Unusual in that it deals with recent history rather than the usual mythic stuff of tragedy, it dramatizes the Greek victory from the perspective of the defeated Persians. The play sets up several clear oppositions between 'Greek' and 'barbarian' ideology, although it should be noted that this is not simply a schema of Greek = good, barbarian = bad, but a more complex development of associations.

A feature common to many Athenian treatments of 'barbarians', including Persians, was the concept that barbarian subjects were slaves to their king, something abhorrent to the Athenian democratic mentality. A caveat here: some care should be exercised when discussing democracy in Greece. Athens, from which most of our literature survives, was a democracy, but not in the way we understand it today. It was very much a slave-owning society and political activity was open to male citizens only. Furthermore, most fifth-century Greek states were not democracies. Oligarchy (rule by a few) and Tyranny (absolute rule by a single man, without necessarily implying the negative connotations of the modern word 'tyranny') were common forms of government. A tyrant could come to power by overthrowing the established government if he had enough popular support. Sparta had two kings.

Bearing this in mind, let us now return to *Seven*. This dramatizes a war of Greeks against Greeks but there are several subtle ways in which the attackers are cast as barbarians. It was noted above that the threat of fire to Thebes would probably have recalled the burning of Athens by the Persians in 480 BC for a contemporary audience, and under this analogy Thebes is comparable to Athens under siege from a barbarian invader.[40] Although the attackers in *Seven* are not barbarians, there is a conscious association made between the attacking army and a foreign or barbarian horde. Early on in the play, the attacking army is described as an enemy 'of alien speech' (170), the primary meaning of the Greek word 'barbarian', which could be used to describe anyone who spoke an unintelligible language. Of course, even if the attackers spoke a different dialect, they certainly did speak Greek, so this is apparently a purposeful decision to characterize them as 'barbarians'. This is consolidated by the suggestion that the attackers represent a threat to the city's altars, gods and rites when Eteocles calls on the citizens of Thebes 'never to let [the rites of their native gods] be obliterated' in the prologue. Such violence against the city's shrines is not something one should expect from an invading force which worships and reveres the same gods as the Thebans. The suggestion, of course, foreshadows the attackers' associations with primeval powers and their general blasphemies, but it also suggests, once again, an alien quality about them.

There is one attacker particularly characterized as barbarian: Eteoclus. This is all the more intriguing because of his hazy status as a mythological figure and, of course, the similarity between his name and that of Eteocles. Eteoclus is a substitute for Adrastus, king of Argos and one of the Seven in other versions. Since Adrastus survived the expedition against Thebes, Aeschylus, by replacing him, can present the complete destruction of the attacking force. As the substitute for the leader who would have been Eteocles' counterpart in rank and status, it has been suggested that Eteoclus is a 'mirror-image' for Eteocles.[41] Little is known about Eteoclus, and indeed, little detail is given about him in *Seven*. He is not a regular figure among the champions who attack Thebes and some scholars have suggested that Aeschylus invented this character, though this is uncertain.[42] At the very least, however, we can be sure that Aeschylus exploited the figure of Eteoclus for his own purposes.

He is characterized through his horses who are said to 'whistle in a barbarian manner' through their 'proud nostrils' (463-4).[43] 'Against this man too', warns the Scout, 'you must send someone who can be relied on to keep off the yoke of slavery from the city' (470-1). Circling on his barbarian horses, he represents the threat of slavery to the city. This is exactly what Eteocles had feared when he prayed that the free land and city of Cadmus never be bound with the yokestrap of slavery (74-5). The polarity between slavery and freedom is evident here. The concept is also repeated later in the words of the

Scout, returned to relay the news of the salvation of Thebes: 'This city has escaped the yoke of slavery' (793). The image of enslavement under the yoke of the enemy ties in clearly with an identification of the attackers as barbarians. In Aeschylus' *Persians*, the image of the yoke as a metaphor for slavery, which is shaken off by Greece, is powerfully exploited.[44] Here also in *Seven*, the yoke can be seen in a similar, if less explicit, context.

Another generic 'barbarian' trait in the Greek mind was wealth in gold. Although fifth-century Greece had productive silver mines, gold was not a resource found on home soil, and, therefore was very much associated with barbarians, who were presented as corrupted by their wealth, as exemplified once again by Aeschylus' *Persians*.[45] Two of the attackers have symbols on their shields explicitly made of gold. Both inscriptions on the shields of Capaneus and Polynices are said to be written in gold, and Polynices' shield also depicts the warrior, who is a figurative representation of himself, cast in gold. This shows that Polynices has been corrupted by a greed for wealth and material possessions, and that the attackers as a force are reminiscent of the Persian king Xerxes' 'gold-adorned army' (*Persians* 9). Indeed, it has been argued, on different grounds, that the central cause of the struggle between the two brothers is each one's desire for material possessions.[46]

5

Women

Warriors and war are certainly the central focus of *Seven*, but the genre of Greek tragedy was notable in antiquity for giving women a voice, although, as we saw in Chapter 1, tragedies were written, produced, and performed by men only, and men were certainly the primary spectators. Like almost every society on earth before recent times, fifth-century BC Athens was a society in which women were excluded from public life. They did not count as citizens, were unrepresented in democratic bodies such as the assembly (*ekklêsia*) or the council (*boulê*), and were unable to do jury service or give testimony in court. Women could be part of public life as market-sellers or courtesans, but respectable women were expected to remain at home, out of the public eye, except during certain approved activities, such as female participation in religious festivals. In this context, it is striking that females have such a strong presence on the Attic stage, and that most Greek tragedies explore the relationship between male and female to a greater or lesser degree.[1] Gender relations are important in Aeschylean tragedy. In the *Oresteia*, Clytemnestra has 'a woman's heart of manly counsel'. The *Suppliant Women* has the Chorus of the daughters of Danaus as the central character of the play, constructed in relation to two father-figures (Danaus and Pelasgus, the Argive king with whom they seek refuge).[2] In *Prometheus Bound* a contrast is established between the immobile Prometheus and the pursued Io.

The situation in *Seven* is also noteworthy. If we discount the inauthentic ending, with the insertion of Antigone and Ismene, we are left with a clear dichotomy between male characters and female Chorus. The atmosphere of war and the threat to Thebes emphasize the different preoccupations and roles of women and warriors in society. This chapter will analyse the identity of the Chorus, and its implications for our under-standing of their behaviour, and will question the assumption, supported by many scholars but not all, that Eteocles' misogy-nistic treatment of the Chorus is justified or appropriate.[3]

Choral identity

The Chorus in Greek tragedy represent a collective character, but also serve certain particular functions. From a structural point of view, their lyric odes form interludes in the action of the play, often reflecting on the situation at hand. As an internal audience to the drama, the Chorus also act as a foil for the spectators' sympathy. We react to their reaction to events. Their collective identity, of course, influences the way they respond to developments.[4] The Chorus of *Seven* are Theban maidens,[5] and their virginal presence creates a stark contrast to the relentless grimness of the warriors. The direct contrast between the maidens and the warriors is emphasized in their opening song, where their maiden supplication of the gods is juxtaposed with the image of 'a wave of men, their crests at an angle ... raised up by the blasts of Ares' (110-15). Indeed the contrast is well captured by the cover image of this volume. Although Tydeus putting Ismene to the sword belongs to an alternative tradition, the image illustrates the helplessness of a maiden against these ferocious warriors.

In terms of transitions and rites of passage, the life of a woman in ancient Greece was fulfilled only through marriage and ultimately the birth of her first child.[6] The threats of abduction, rape, and enslavement which face the maidens thus represent not only the horrific plight of the women of a conquered city, but also the abrupt severance of a normal tran-sition to fulfilment.[7] The Chorus' fear of such a fate is graphically expressed in the second choral song (first stasimon) where they imagine the city's women being taken captive 'both young and old, dragged by their hair like horses, their clothes being torn off, and the city crying out as it is emptied of this wretched plunder from which rises a mingled clamour' (328-31). The presentation of the conquered city's women as possessions, plunder, like horses, to be carried off and disposed of at will, could not be clearer. But a preoccupation with this fate continues into the next strophe: 'it is lamentable when those just reared are plucked unripe and traverse, before the lawful time, a hateful path away from their homes: I declare that even the dead fare better than they do' (332-7). The cumulative effect of the sentiment expressed by the Chorus is this: it is a grim fate for women of any age to be taken captive and enslaved, but it is especially pitiable when this fate befalls unmarried maidens like us; indeed death would be preferable.

This concept of death as preferable to enslavement and concubinage is one expressed elsewhere in Greek tragedy. The Trojan maiden Polyxena, who is sacrificed at the tomb of Achilles, concludes that death is a more fortunate fate than enslavement (Euripides *Hecuba*, 367ff.), and she is envied by other captive Trojan women (e.g. by Andromache in Euripides' *Trojan Women*, 679-80). So, the Chorus' identity is crucial for heightening the impact of the great threat which looms against Thebes. But the Chorus maidens also represent the sterility of Thebes while the descendant of Laius continues to hold power. Not yet in a position to bear legitimate offspring, they are essentially the representatives of the citizen body, and are a metaphor for the city of Thebes itself, unable to produce healthy offspring until the right time, which for Thebes means the time at which the house of Laius becomes extinct.

Eteocles' misogyny

It is through Eteocles' interaction with the Chorus maidens that his misogynistic streak is exposed. The diametric opposition of Eteocles to the Chorus in *Seven* has long been noted, as has the parallelism between the two scenes of debate between them.[8] It has even been argued that all Aeschylean drama structures itself around an opposition of male and female.[9] But gender relations are particularly strained in *Seven*. When Eteocles re-enters after the opening choral song, he launches into a bitter invective against women. He calls the Chorus 'insufferable creatures' (181) who 'cry and howl in a way that would be abhorrent to sensible people' (186). 'Whether in bad times or in welcome prosperity', continues Eteocles, 'may I not share my household with the female race! When a woman is doing well, her brazenness is unbearable to live with; when she's frightened, she is an even greater evil to family and city' (187-90). He accuses the Chorus of panic-mongering, and of doing their best to advance the enemy cause, resulting in the city being sacked from within by its own people (194). 'That's the sort of thing you'll get if you live with women!' he says (195). Such claims are clearly exaggerations, and it is evident that Eteocles does not seriously regard the Chorus as an 'enemy within'. He certainly never describes them as enemies, but he does feel very strongly that the Chorus are acting out of place. 'Out-of-doors affairs are the concern of men; women are not to offer opinions about them. Stay inside and do no harm!' (200-1). His rage and anger towards the Chorus are in marked contrast to the calm and calculating disposition he later displays in the shield scene, and the crucial question in analysing Eteocles' behaviour towards the Chorus is: is his misogyny justified, even in an ancient context?[10]

There are several issues to consider here and the matter is not straightforward. What is most difficult, of course, is to estimate how an original audience might be expected to respond to this, but there are some clues. A striking feature of Eteocles' invective is not just his reproach of the Chorus, but his *complete rejection* of the female race (*genos*). Other tragic characters voice misogynistic views. Jason in Euripides' *Medea* claims that the world would be rid of all its troubles if only men could find some way to reproduce without women (*Medea* 573-5), and Hippolytus in Euripides' play of that name voices similar views in a lengthy speech, declaring women to be a curse on the world (*Hippolytus* 617-68). One famous Aeschylean passage claims that the father alone generates the offspring while the mother simply nurtures it (*Eumenides* 657-61). But there are specific reasons for these suggestions in each case. Jason is trying to argue (though not terribly convincingly) that it is not for lust that he is leaving Medea for the princess of Corinth, but because he wants royal Corinthian children as siblings for his children from Medea to ensure them all prosperity. Hippolytus' invective is provoked by the unwelcome news that his step-mother is lusting after him, and he is ultimately punished for his disregard of the female sex and of the goddess Aphrodite. In *Eumenides*, the god Apollo is trying to argue that Orestes is not, in essence, the offspring of his mother, in order to clear him of the crime of matricide which Apollo himself had prescribed.

In the case of Eteocles, however, his rejection of the female *genos* ties in with his rejection of his own *genos* in favour of association with the *polis* (discussed in Chapter 2). His genealogy, which makes his mother the same figure as his grandmother, reveals women as incestuous, abhorrent crea-tures. That the incest was committed in ignorance does not affect its outcome, and there may have been negative associa-tions with the character of Jocasta developed in the previous plays of the trilogy. So, Eteocles wishes specifically not to share his household with a woman and sees a frightened woman as a threat to her *family* first, and *polis* second (190). This reinforces both the strong association between female and family, but also the female's subordinate position in *polis* life.

Rejection of the female *genos* again highlights the sterility of Thebes, associated with the family curse. Before the incest of Oedipus and Jocasta is discovered, Thebes is plagued with sterility, at least in the Sophoclean version of events. Rejection of women, we note, is particular to Eteocles, who invokes only virgin goddesses.[11] Polynices has married the daughter of Adrastus while in exile. This may have been a political alliance, but such a basis for marriage was common in antiquity, and although there is no reference to any offspring from the union, there is not necessarily any denial of offspring either. The word 'childless' used to describe the brothers at 828 is textually corrupt and all of lines 822-31 are suspected of being later additions.[12] Thersander, Polynices' son, is already mentioned in Pindar's *Second Olympian* (dated 476). Polynices' status as a married man creates a contrast to the misogyny of his brother. Indeed, it is difficult to see what basis Eteocles has to suggest that women in prosperity are just as unbearable as women under threat. Does he have any experience of dealing with women in prosperity? Certainly none is suggested in the play. So, Eteocles' outright rejection of womankind is presented as unnatural and excessive, even if some of his reproaches against the Chorus are justified.

A certain justification of his anger against the Chorus may be seen in his condemnation of their panic-mongering. He is surely right to claim that the Chorus' hysteria will do nothing to help resistance against the attackers. But again here he is arguing against nature, attempting to suppress the instinct of the Chorus. Bearing in mind that the average age for a girl to marry in classical Greece was fourteen or fifteen, the Chorus maidens are to be thought of as around thirteen years old, on the cusp of marriageable age. We can readily deduce from the mythical history of Thebes that these girls have never yet experienced the besieging of their city, and their reaction to it is very much in keeping with the cast of their character. The panic felt by the Chorus is expressed through the disorganized astrophic lyrics of the opening song, but their *motivation* in coming to the shrines of the gods is, in fact, entirely appropriate to the situation. In times of war, it is a fundamental role of women to conduct appropriate ritual worship of the city's gods. When Hector comes back from battle, and finds his wife Andromache is not at home, he expects her to be either with her sister-in-law or worshipping Athena (*Iliad* 6.376-80). And this brings us back to Eteocles' remark that women should stay indoors where they can do no harm. He is right that 'out-of-doors affairs are the concern of men'. Respectable women should not be out and about in inappropriate circumstances, but ritual worship is *not* one of those circumstances. Again, his response to the Chorus is revealed as too harsh.[13]

In fact, every aspect of Eteocles' speech here is excessive. His suggestion that the Chorus' panic will cause the city to be 'sacked from within' is antithetical to the presentation of the fearless defenders who will be summoned to Thebes' aid. On the one hand he discounts the Chorus, and on the other he assumes that they will have a great impact on the city's morale. But perhaps most telling is the death threat he expresses not just against women, but against 'man or woman or anything in between' who fails to obey his command (196-7); 'a vote of death will be passed against them and there is no way they will escape execution by public stoning' (198-9). The reference to a vote here exploits the language of Athenian democracy, where a majority vote would hold sway, but Eteocles has absolute rule and the implication is that his vote will be the only one to count. He thus represents the antithesis of Athenian democracy, and demonstrates an aggressive attitude not just towards women, but to any who disobey him. The nature of the punishment is also excessive. Death by stoning was a punishment reserved only for the most abhorrent crimes like high treason.[14] Eteocles is truly a member of his own *genos*. Though we cannot tell how other family members were presented in the two preceding plays, an interesting parallel with the Sophoclean Oedipus (in *Oedipus the King*) and Creon (in *Antigone*) suggests itself. Both of these utter excessive threats, Oedipus against Creon (Jocasta's brother, Eteocles' uncle), Tiresias the prophet, and eventually even against the Chorus of male elders, and Creon in *Antigone* threatens Antigone, his niece, and Haemon, his son and Antigone's fiancé. In this context we can observe a pattern of expressing inappropriate and excessive threats of violence, not only as a characteristic of the tyrant,[15] but as a family trait in the *genos* of Eteocles.

The action of the Chorus in seeking protection from the gods was, we said, appropriate, but what about their terrified frenzy? Here again, their identity may provide some explanation. As pubescent females, these Chorus maidens could easily be expected to act somewhat irrationally when threatened with such terrible danger. They do not have the life experience of a

Clytemnestra or a Penelope, who can keep their cool while under duress. The behaviour of the Chorus, while perhaps not admirable, is in keeping with their identity as maidens. Eteocles' invective against women in general seems not to recognize this, and one suspects that even in classical Greece where the male was held in higher regard than the female, a contemporary audience would have found Eteocles' attitude excessive.

So vicious is his attack on the Chorus that they are shocked into silence. Ironically Eteocles, whose aim is to silence them (cf. 232 'your business is to keep quiet and stay in your homes'), is the one to make them break their silence, asking contemptuously: 'Did you hear me or not? Or am I speaking to the deaf?' (202). In addressing him in their opening response as 'dear son of Oedipus' (203), the Chorus remind him directly of the *genos* he has rejected. From here there is a gradual turnaround in gender relations. The whole exchange of 203-44 is marked by the difference in register between the worried Chorus, who sing their lines in emotional dochmiacs, and Eteocles who responds pedantically in the iambic trimeters used of ordinary speech. As the exchange develops, Eteocles is ultimately forced to acknowledge that the Chorus are acting appropriately in honouring the gods. He tries to suggest that women have no part in worshipping the gods, arguing that offering *sphagia* ('slaughtered sacrifices') to the gods 'is the business of men' (230), but this does not invalidate the propriety of women worshipping the gods when their city is besieged. In fact, this is one of the prime roles of women in war as exemplified by Hector's advice to the women of Troy to do exactly that (*Iliad* 6.286-311). Eteocles must modify his approach to the women in order to avoid saying that their worshipping the gods is wrong. 'I don't at all resent your honouring the race of gods,' he backtracks, qualifying this with a caveat not to get excessively frightened (236-8).

When the Chorus continue to express their fear, Eteocles is again disdainful towards women as a race (256), but the choral response emphasizes the equal wretchedness of men and women alike in a conquered city (257). Eteocles ignores the sentiment and reproaches the Chorus for, once more, uttering ill-omened words concerning the capture of the city. He is right about this, particularly since the Chorus are touching the images of the gods, giving their words extra force (258). But after the shield scene, the Chorus and Eteocles will end up in a curiously reversed situation. The Chorus will be the ones attempting to calm his emotions and prevent him from being carried off by his delusion (677-8). At that point too, the Chorus will have stopped panicking about the possibility of subjugation and will settle their attention on the family curse. There is no question of an exchange of gender associations. It is not that Eteocles is feminized in any way, as male characters sometimes are in Greek tragedy, nor that the Chorus take on some kind of masculine role. The specific fear is that Eteocles is being carried off by male 'spear-mad' delusion (687-8), and the Chorus conform to the stereotypical female role of persuader.

It is strange that the adolescent Chorus address Eteocles as 'child' (685). This has often worried scholars, leading one to suggest that the Chorus are, in fact, made up of old women.[16] But their designation of Eteocles as 'child' fulfils two functions. It reminds the audience of Eteocles' position within his *genos*, as the child of an abhorrent and incestuous union, and it also represents an attempt by the Chorus to become effective persuaders. They plead with Eteocles: 'be persuaded by us women, even if it is hateful to you' (712). Women in Greek literature are particularly skilled at persuading men, but in *Seven* the women fail to persuade Eteocles not to go against his brother. There are several reasons for their failure. Women who are successful in persuasion tend to be married, mature women or divine forces: Clytemnestra, Medea, Penelope, Circe, Calypso. Here again, the identity of the Chorus as adolescent girls is important. They attempt to become more effective persuaders by setting themselves up as mature in relation to Eteocles the 'child', but this is untenable and fails. Another factor is at work here also – the force of the Curse, which has now been set in motion. Eteocles is no longer a man like Agamemnon, Creon, the Suitors, or Odysseus, to be manipulated by a female. He has become a sword personified, as indicated by his expression 'I am whetted, your words will not blunt me' (715).

Speech vs. silence

Female speech in Greek tragedy has been the focus of some scholarly attention in recent years, most notably by Laura McClure in her book *Spoken Like a Woman*. She does not deal with *Seven* in detail, but does suggest that the Chorus' identity as young women of child-bearing age in *Seven* presents them as a threat to masculine authority in the context of classical Athens where reforms had been introduced to restrict the role of lamentation to older women.[17] However, McClure's general hypothesis, that women had licence to public expression in certain circumstances such as prayer and lamentation, is nonetheless applicable to the situation in *Seven*, and a mythical context need not necessarily be read against contemporary Athenian legislation.

Throughout the interaction between Eteocles and the Chorus, he tries to silence them, unsuccessfully. His frustration escalates as his own words fail to have any effect. His question 'will you not keep quiet, instead of airing it all in public?' (250) raises the issue of appropriateness once more. Implicit in his words is the suggestion that women should not be speaking in public as the Chorus are. The public arena is the domain of men, the private sphere the realm of women. 'Can't you put up with it in silence, confound you?' Eteocles continues (252), but in each case the Chorus completely ignore him. Their lines in this stichomythic exchange consist of prayers to the gods which betray no indication that they have even heard Eteocles. It is only at his final 'Be silent, you poor fool'(262) that they respond directly and in the way he wants: 'I'll be silent' (263).

Eteocles has achieved his aim. But after all this fuss to get the Chorus to keep quiet, arguing that they should go home, and only barely acknowledging their right and role to honour the city's gods, Eteocles immediately asks them to keep speaking, praying, and crying forth. There is, of course, a fundamental difference in *the way* Eteocles wishes the Chorus to speak. They are to 'utter a better prayer' (266); he means one based on reciprocity, promising the gods good worship if they help Thebes, rather than simply begging the gods for aid. We have seen, in Chapter 3, how the Chorus remind the gods of past worship, but Eteocles wants them to emphasize future worship as dependent on success. They must 'then utter the sacred, auspicious ululation of triumph, the customary Hellenic cry at sacrifices, to inspire friends and dispel their fear of the foe' (267-70). Eteocles' instructions in themselves acknowledge the importance of the female voice in a manner which ties into the gradual reversal of roles mentioned above. The ululation (*ololugmos*) is a sacrificial cry specifically associated with women and expressing joy and triumph. Elsewhere in Aeschylus the female *ololugmos* is associated with perverted sacrifice and signals doom (*Agamemnon* 28, 595, *Libation Bearers* 396). These plays post-date *Seven* but they present a noteworthy parallel nonetheless. It is, after all, directly after Eteocles' instruction to utter the *ololugmos* that he strides off to station six men, with himself as the seventh – a decision which will be his own doom.

In any case, the Chorus do not raise an *ololugmos*. After Eteocles' departure, their opening words acknowledge his instructions but continue to betray their fear: 'I heed your words, but terror will not let my soul sleep' (286-7). However, there is a marked shift in speech patterns, namely that the function of relaying the noise of the besieging army moves from the Chorus to the Scout and is anticipated by Eteocles' words on his exit which he wishes to make 'before a messenger comes with a flurry of hasty, noisy words and causes a crisis that sets all ablaze' (285-6). His final words are very telling. They reveal the validity of the Chorus' worries and the accuracy of their presentation of the atmosphere in Thebes during their opening ode. The hasty, noisy, crisis-causing words of the male messenger are just as worrisome as those of the Chorus, but in the case of the messenger, Eteocles has no recourse to condemnation through misogyny.

The difference, of course, is that the Scout, when he arrives, speaks with the authority of an eyewitness, and the Chorus might be accused of exaggerating what they are hearing. But is the content of the *parodos* so different from the report of the Scout? We saw in Chapter 4 how the noises made by the attackers are stressed in the shield scene, and this is also one of the main features of the *parodos*. Furthermore, the Chorus are careful to construct their intimations in terms of what they see as well as what they hear. Not only do they hear the 'great host of horses pouring forth at a gallop' (80), 'roaring like an irresistible mountain torrent' (85-6), but they also see the dust rising in the air 'a voiceless messenger but true and certain' (81-2). They hear the clatter of shields and the clatter of spears (100, 103). The sensation is so vivid, that they can claim to *see* the noise (103). They hear the piercing whine of the horses' bit (122-3), 'the rattle of chariots around the city ... the sockets of their heavy-laden axels squealing' (151-3), 'the bombardment of stones on the battlements' (158) and 'the clashing of bronze-rimmed shields at the gates' (160). It has been shown that sound is used here to create off stage space.[18]

The image conveyed in the *parodos* is of a large attacking horde, while the shield scene focuses on seven individual champions. But the emphasis on the terrifying quantity of this force is the same in each case. The reactions of the speakers are different. The Chorus are hysterical, the Scout is fearful but collected. But we have already seen that the choral reaction to the situation is in keeping with their identity. What a comparison between the two treatments of the attackers stresses is that, in spite of Eteocles' frustrations, the Chorus' fears are not exaggerated but very real.

The second choral ode (first stasimon) has a similar theme to the first. It expresses fear at the imagined destruction of the city. The overriding sense conveyed by this song is one of tumultuous confusion and a wretched fate, but the focus on noise is gone. The third choral song (second stasimon) has as its subject the family curse, an issue which also pervades the fourth and final choral songs (the third stasimon and the antiphonal dirge), both of which lament the dead princes. Here we witness another way in which the female voice in classical Greece had a significant role in society. Lamentation over the dead was one of the primary public female functions in classical Greece. Indeed, the opening choral song can also be read as a lament, though it is ill-omened, this time a lament for (the anticipation of) a fallen city.[19]

However, the Chorus' lament over the dead brothers is not what one might typically expect. The Chorus as chief mourners are unusual in being unrelated to the deceased, and having even been despised by one of them. Even if one includes the spurious ending containing the sisters Antigone and Ismene, the Chorus remain the leaders of the lament. As we saw in Chapter 1, this is one of several factors which confirms that the ending is inauthentic. It would be highly inappropriate for the sisters to be present but in a subsidiary mourning position. However, if the death of the brothers means the extinction of the house, then there are no appropriate females to lament them, and the Chorus take on this role more convincingly.

The choral song has the form of a typical lament, but its content is disturbing. A traditional lament for fallen warriors would naturally be a kind of eulogy recalling glorious deeds and military prowess. In *Seven*, however, the Chorus' lament is injected with disapproval for the brothers' actions. Their battle was ill-omened (838-9), the brothers were foolish (875), they sent the walls of their house crashing in ruin (881-2), they are not a source of pride for their mother but one of ill-fortune (926-8). Language of victory is exploited to describe the disasters which have befallen the house, a perversion of appropriate lament. The brothers have 'adorned their family with many sorrows', the Curses have shrilled their cry of triumph over their bodies, and the trophy of Atê stands at the gate where they were killed (951-60).[20]

The content of the lament fits the context of the play. That both brothers are blamed in the lament confirms their dual responsibility, but in the context of *Seven* it is difficult to see

how a eulogy for either brother could be composed. This is reinforced by the final lines of the lament which raise the issue of
the brothers' final resting place. It is suggested that the
brothers be buried in the place of greatest honour (1003), but it
will be a pain to their father if they are to be interred beside him
(1004). Again, we see that a normal and auspicious course of
action, to be buried alongside one's family, will not work for this
particular *genos*. This is where the authentic text ends. It must
have been followed by some resolution as to where the brothers
ought to be buried before the exit in a funeral procession.[21]

The end of *Seven* reveals the importance of female speech
and the ultimate foresight of the Chorus. Although their speech
may have been ill omened at the beginning of the play, once they
have calmed down, their predictions are revealed as true.[22]
Throughout, their invocation of the gods is important for the
city's protection. But the Chorus seem to undergo a maturing
process during the course of the play. The young and inexperi-
enced virgins of the play's opening have been sobered by the
reality of the fratricidal slaughter which has taken place in spite
of their protestations. True, they failed in their attempts to
persuade Eteocles, but their understanding and recognition of
the workings of the Curse link them to prophetic virginal
priestesses like Cassandra in Aeschylus' *Agamemnon*.[23] There,
the situation is reversed: the Chorus of old men fail to understand the prophetic words of the young maiden. In *Seven*, it is
more that the male fails to heed than to understand, but female
speech follows a parallel pattern in recounting the various
generations of the family curse down to the current dramatic
time, which both Cassandra in *Agamemnon* and the Chorus in
Seven do.

Speech and silence are each appropriate in different circumstances. So the Curse in *Seven* is at times silent (897) at times
shrieking (953-4). That the Chorus' speech is specifically
gendered is indicated by their first word *threumai* 'I cry out', a
verb used only of female speech.[24] When the Chorus express
themselves, it is always on an occasion appropriate for females.
They appeal to the gods when the city is besieged, they wish

victory to the city's defenders and death to their foe, they attempt to prevent Eteocles from doing battle with his brother, and they recount the family curse and lament its fulfilment. The content of their speech (or song) can appear inappropriate but can be explained by its context. The excessive fears of the Chorus at the beginning are perhaps ill omened, but they are justified over and over again by the enormous threat of the attackers which is emphasized in so many different ways. Similarly the emphasis on disaster in their lament for the brothers reflects the reality of the house of Thebes.

In the shadow of Homer

We have already noted several ways in which the *Iliad* is a significant model against which to contextualize *Seven*. Both works deal with a city under siege from an invading army. So *Iliad* 6 has been informative for analysing the appropriate roles of women during war, but we have not yet explored this context to its full potential. In *Iliad* 6 (431-9), Andromache had pleaded with Hector to give up his quest for glory in battle.[25] But she is unable to persuade him since his regard for the Trojans and his own heart spur him on to fight in the front line and seek glory (*Iliad* 6.440-6). The Chorus in *Seven*, like Andromache, disparage the warrior's quest for glory when they tell Eteocles that 'god values even an inglorious victory' (716), meaning a victory in which Eteocles does not gain glory. Eteocles' response, however, is predictably curt and dismissive, very different from the measured and considered response of Hector to Andromache. Eteocles simply blusters: 'That's not a suggestion that a man-at-arms should tolerate' (717). The outcome of both female intercessions is the same, but the way in which this comes about highlights the great difference in the attitudes of Hector and Eteocles towards women. For Hector they are to be revered and respected, for Eteocles they are to be silenced and repressed.

There are other Iliadic parallels. The attackers are distinguished collectively in *Seven* as Achaeans and Argives, as we noted in Chapter 4, names used to designate the Greeks attacking Troy in the *Iliad*. This casts the women of Thebes as Trojan women under siege and intensifies the parallels discussed above. Some of the scenes imagined by the Chorus recall Iliadic ones. During the shield scene, each of the choral responses to the threat at every gate contains a curse against the attacker(s) and/or a prayer for the defender/the city. Gradually, the Chorus abandon their anticipation of destruction in these responses, but this concern is still very much apparent in the first two instances. In response to Capaneus, the Chorus imagine that he will abduct them from their maiden homes if the thunderbolt doesn't stop him, and in response to Tydeus, the Chorus 'tremble to see the bloody deaths of men who perish fighting for their dear ones' (419-21). This image cannot but bring to mind the death of Hector, whose love for his family is made so clear in the *Iliad* and whose graphic death is described in such detail in *Iliad* 22. Similarly the image conveyed in the second choral ode of 'loud, bloody screams rising up from infants fresh from the nourishing breast' (349-51) recalls the taking of Troy which involved the massacre of all infants and children including, famously, Hector's son Astyanax. This happens outside the narrative timeframe of the *Iliad*, but was well known from other epics dealing with the Trojan cycle. The effect of casting Thebes as an imaginary Troy justifies the Chorus' fears and confirms that Eteocles' abusive attitude towards them is excessive.

6

The Legacy: Fifth Century BC to Twenty-First Century AD

From all the themes and issues discussed in the earlier chapters of this book, there is one overriding element which links them all – war. The harsh reality of war, especially civil war, is also the main feature in the legacy of *Seven*. This chapter will discuss the fate of the text of the play, its survival, and how it has been viewed. It will look at *Seven*'s influence on other fifth-century tragedies and will discuss the legacy of the fratricidal war which *Seven* dramatizes, and which becomes synthesized with subsequent versions in later receptions.

The popularity and survival of *Seven*

Seven may have been one of Aeschylus' 'most popular and influential plays in the fifth century',[1] but it has remained arguably one of the least popular Greek tragedies from the sixteenth century to recent times. This is partly explained by the survival of Euripides' more popular *Phoenician Women* which uses more naturalistic language and whose plot maintains an exciting pace. Our evidence suggests that Aeschylean tragedy was not much reperformed in the fourth century, although Sophoclean and Euripidean tragedy was.[2] The lofty language of Aeschylean verse and the relatively static stage action of a play like *Seven* may not have appealed much to a Hellenistic audience (*c.* 323-30 BC), who favoured fast-paced dramas often involving mistaken identities, a favourite plot technique of Euripides, and of the Hellenistic comic dramatist Menander.

However the textual transmission of *Seven* does imply that it was a more popular play in antiquity and in medieval times than its later fortunes suggest. *Seven* seems to have been revived in the fourth or early third century BC when the final scene was added to fit in with Sophocles' *Antigone* and Euripides' *Phoenician Women*, as discussed in Chapter 1.[3] It was one of seven Aeschylean tragedies apparently selected for canonization in the early Byzantine period, possibly the fourth century AD, and one of three Aeschylean plays (along with *Prometheus* and *Persians*) which are far better represented than the rest in the medieval manuscript tradition.[4] It is possible that conservative educational systems during the seventh and eighth centuries AD were responsible for the continued transmission of *Seven*.[5] The text of *Seven* survives in several papyrus fragments from the second century, which were preserved in the sands of Oxyrhynchus in Egypt, and in some thirty-three manuscripts dating from the tenth to the fifteenth centuries.[6]

The invention of the printing press in the fifteenth century ensured the survival and increased dissemination of tragic texts, but Aeschylus was the last major Greek author to be published, the reason for this apparently being the difficult language of his plays. It was not until 1518, three years after the death of its founder Aldus Manutius, that the Aldine Press published an *editio princeps*, 'a first edition', of Aeschylus' extant plays, including *Seven*.[7] Similarly, when Greek tragedies were translated into the vernacular and performed, from the sixteenth to the nineteenth centuries, there was a strong preference for the plays of Sophocles and Euripides, with little attention paid to Aeschylus.[8] Early commentaries on Aeschylus' plays, such as that of the Dutch scholar Cornelis de Pauw (published in 1745), were regarded with great contempt by later scholars.[9] Indeed, it was not until the mid-nineteenth century, when philological examination of tragic texts had become a serious academic pursuit, that the authenticity of the final scene in *Seven* was seriously disputed. The German philologist Schöll was the first to suggest the deletion of *Seven* 1005-78, and virtually all recent scholars have agreed (as discussed in Chapter 1).

Critical approaches

Apart from being a subject for rigorous textual criticism, *Seven* has attracted analysis by scholars through various critical approaches. We saw in Chapter 4 how the shield scene has been analysed variously in terms of hermeneutics, semiotics, structuralism, and imagery. The shield scene has also, of course, been subject to textual analysis, notably by the twentieth-century scholar Eduard Fraenkel.[10] Other issues have been the subject of scholarly debate in the history of twentieth-century critical analysis of the play, and it may be useful to synthesize here various critical approaches which have been dealt with in more detail in previous chapters and accompanying notes.

The political background to the plays of Aeschylus was discussed in detail by Podlecki in 1966, and his book on this subject remains the most important treatment of this issue. He highlights, with reference to the political background of *Seven*, the curbed powers of powerful clans in Athenian politics, and persuasively rejects the arguments of Post (published in 1950) who had suggested that *Seven* could be read as political propaganda for the fifth-century Athenian statesman Pericles.[11] Cameron and Thalmann have both discussed the significance of Athenian inheritance law being changed to apportion patrimony equally among sons for the context of *Seven*.[12]

Most hotly debated among scholars, however, has been the issue of how to interpret the character of Eteocles and his treatment of the Chorus. This Companion has supported the minority view, but a view which has found increasing support in recent scholarship, especially in Stehle's 2005 analysis of prayer and curse, that Eteocles is presented as excessive in his treatment of the Chorus and unsympathetic as a character, and that the position of the Chorus is, to a great extent, justified. Limitations of space prevent a separate analysis here of scholarly opinions on this subject, but an excellent overview of major scholarship is already available in Lloyd's introduction to the *Oxford Readings in Aeschylus*.[13] That Eteocles does make real decisions is no longer a real topic of controversy. The work of the scholar Albin Lesky was instrumental in disproving the theory of Solmsen and others, which argued that Eteocles was simply driven along by events outside his control and was not responsible for making decisions.[14] Similarly the theory that Eteocles' death is to be understood as a 'sacrificial death' (an *Opfertod*), formulated by German scholars of the mid-twentieth century, has been largely refuted.[15]

Seven, the play, and the myth of the Seven

We have traced various themes and issues of importance in Aeschylus' *Seven*, including three generations of crime, concepts of human responsibility and free will, the horror of civil war, the presentation of individual arrogance, a corrupted family, and a determination to destroy. All these are explored in various ways and with different emphases in the legacy of the Theban saga, but it must be acknowledged, before embarking on a discussion of the legacy of these themes, that the reception history of *Seven* is impossible to trace in isolation from the reception of the myth it dramatizes. This is essentially true of the legacy of any play of which multiple versions exist. *Medea* is a case in point. Euripides and the Roman tragedian Seneca both wrote influential *Medea* plays, and Apollonius Rhodius' epic *Argonautica*, written in the third century BC also provides a detailed picture of the figure of Medea. Later versions of *Medea* are often influenced by all three of these works.[16]

It is particularly true in the case of *Seven* that the reception of the play cannot be divorced from the legacy of the mythical events it recounts. This is because Euripides' version of the same events as produced in his *Phoenician Women* proved by far the more popular of the two tragedies, and was a strong influence on the *Thebaid*, the epic of the Roman poet Statius, which in turn was an important influence on medieval and later treatments of the 'Seven against Thebes' story. Even those who have written plays directly based on Aeschylus' *Seven*, such as the Cuban playwright Antón Arrufat (discussed at the end in this chapter), have acknowledged a debt to Euripides' version as well as others. Certainly, for a modern theatre audience, a faithful rendition of the Aeschylean text would make for an unfamiliar type of performance, more akin to a long poetic and operatic recital, with a connected plot line, than the kind of dramatic action expected in modern theatre. This chapter will, therefore, trace the legacy of the mythical events which *Seven* dramatizes, the attack on Thebes and the fratricidal death of Eteocles and Polynices, in order to get a broad historical overview of their reception.

Seven and Euripides' *Phoenician Women*

The fifth century BC is the only time in the legacy of the Theban saga that we can analyse the direct reception of *Seven*, in particular through Euripides' *Phoenician Women*. This is clearest in the presentation of shield emblems in *Phoenician Women* (1104-40), an obvious reaction to the shield scene in *Seven*. Amphiaraus' shield is blank as in *Seven*, but the shield emblems of the other champions differ on significant levels. Parthenopaeus' shield displays his mother Atalanta overwhelming the boar of Aitolia with her bow. Where in *Seven* he bore a symbol to threaten Thebes specifically, associated with Theban history, in *Phoenician Women* he bears the symbol of his own family. Hippomedon bears Panoptes, an epithet of a certain herdsman Argus who had been instructed by Hera to keep watch over Io (one of Zeus' many conquests). The choice of the name is important. It means 'the many-eyed' and is qualified by the explanation that Panoptes sees all the time, some of his eyes working in the day, some in the night (1113-18). The emblem suggests a capping of the shield symbol of the Aeschylean Tydeus. His full moon was 'the eye of Night' implying that he had no real vision in the daytime, and coincided with the Aeschylean Tydeus' rejection of Amphiaraus' prophetic vision.

Euripides' Tydeus has a shield covered with a lion skin. His lion skin reminds us of a powerful but primitive warrior, like Heracles, who slew the Nemean lion with his club and then donned the skin as a trophy. But, more significantly, he carries a firebrand in his hand intending to burn the city, thus becoming the embodiment of the shield symbol of the Aeschylean Capaneus.[17] Parthenopaeus later represents a further stage of this embodiment when he 'shouts fire and destruction' on the city (1154-5). He physically shouts where in Aeschylus it is the silent image on the shield of Capaneus that paradoxically 'shouts' through the written inscription (*Seven* 434). Polynices' shield displays Potniad colts, running and crazed. This picks up the imagery of the crazed horses lusting for war in Aeschylus' *Seven*, particularly the horses of Eteoclus. Capaneus bears an earth-born giant who has wrested a whole city from its foundations and carries it on his shoulders. The image of the giant is no longer Capaneus himself, as at *Seven* 424, but is here transferred to his shield, an indication of his arrogance. Adrastus (replacing Aeschylus' Eteoclus) bears a shield emblem of one hundred snakes. The snakes on the shield are carrying off the children of the Cadmeans in their jaws. This combines the Typhon of Aeschylus' Hippomedon with the Sphinx of his Parthenopaeus. But Adrastus' snakes do not simply breathe out smoke like Aeschylus' Typhon, they actively snatch and carry off the Thebans in their jaws. In Aeschylus, one Sphinx could carry off one Theban, but a hundred-headed snake can snatch away scores of Thebans at a time. The Euripidean image once again caps the Aeschylean one.

All or some of these lines have been suspected by several scholars of being an interpolation into the Euripidean text by a fourth-century author. It is suggested, among other things, that the style of the language is not of the quality one would usually expect from Euripides. There is some support for this view, but the authenticity of these lines has also been defended, and it is very tempting to see them as genuine Euripides precisely because they respond to Aeschylus in a conscious way, something typically Euripidean.[18] In any case, the issue does not affect our purpose here. Whether they are genuine Euripides or a later interpolation, the lines still constitute a direct reception of the shield scene in *Seven*.[19]

Other, more minor, echoes of *Seven* can be heard in Euripides' *Phoenician Women*. The servant's concern with appropriate female behaviour when Antigone takes her place on the walls of Thebes to observe the army gathering below may recall Eteocles' concern for appropriate female behaviour in *Seven*, though the manifestation of the invaders through sound in *Seven* is here replaced with vision. The scene is known as the *teichoskopia* or 'observation from the city walls' and is inspired by its epic prede- cessor in *Iliad* 3. Statius (discussed below), in book seven of his epic *Thebaid*, also includes a *teichoskopia* by Antigone.

The reference to the etymology of Polynices' name as meaning 'Much-strife' at 636-7 recalls the exploitation of this etymology in *Seven* (576-8), and the recurring imagery of iron harks back to the insistent references to iron in the last third of *Seven*.[20] But there are, of course, serious innovations on Euripides' part. Jocasta and Oedipus are both still alive, and Jocasta attempts to reconcile the brothers. They agree to a truce and Polynices enters the city to negotiate with Eteocles but these negotiations fail, mainly because of Eteocles. Polynices is depicted favourably. Eteocles has broken a previous sworn pact to share the rule of Thebes with his brother for alternate periods of time. The irony of Polynices, the man 'of much strife', being more virtuous than Eteocles, the man 'of true glory' is a typical Euripidean touch. In other plays too he explores the ironies of etymologies and paradoxical names.[21] Other innovations here include the introduction of a duel between the brothers, separate from the first assault of the Seven, to settle matters, resulting in their mutual slaughter, and the self-sacrifice of Creon's son Menoeceus, whose death is prophesied to bring the favour of Ares and Thebes' salvation.

Seven and other fifth-century tragedies

There are several other extant fifth-century tragedies which post-date *Seven* and are of some relevance to the legacy of the

play and the myth it dramatizes: three plays by Sophocles –
Antigone, Oedipus the King, and *Oedipus at Colonus* – and one
play by Euripides – *Suppliant Women*. The three Sophoclean
plays, although often called 'the Theban trilogy' were produced
separately during different periods of Sophocles' life. The relationship between *Seven* and *Antigone* is extremely unusual in
that it works in both directions. It has been a premise of this
Companion that the ending of our transmitted text of *Seven* is
an appendage, added to make *Seven* conform to the Sophoclean
epilogue dramatized in his *Antigone*. The arguments in favour
of this, as we saw in Chapter 1, are certainly persuasive. Indeed
if we take the ending as genuine, then *Antigone* loses much of
its impact since its plot would be so clearly based on the ending
of *Seven*.

Scholars have detected a more subtle influence of *Seven* on
Antigone. In the choral entry song of *Antigone*, which remem-
bers the attack of the Seven on Thebes, it is suggested that the
attackers were defeated because of their boasts against Zeus,
their wealth in gold, and their large numbers (127-33), echoing
Aeschylean treatment in *Seven*. Imagery of madness, fire, and
breathing (134-40) is again familiar from *Seven* as is the equal
share of death apportioned to the brothers (144-7). The third
choral song in *Antigone* (582-625) which deals with the cycle of
disasters afflicting the house of Thebes seems inspired by the
third choral song of *Seven* (720-91). The importance of the term
atê 'delusion' in both choruses (and discussed in Chapter 3)
provides a crucial link, and in each case, the unending 'storm'
of troubles is presented as continuing until the family is wiped
out. A final point of comparison between the two plays is the
graphic recollection of the incest of which Antigone, Ismene and
their brothers are products, brought into sharp relief when
Antigone emotionally laments the 'horrors of the maternal bed'
and the incestuous union of her parents (863-71; cf. 49-57).[22]

Of course, the gruesome reality of the incest is something
which also features strongly in Sophocles' *Oedipus the King*
once the truth has finally been revealed. Oedipus in a rage
exclaims: 'Give me a sword, I say, to find this wife that is no

wife, this mother's womb, this field of double sowing whence I sprang and where I sowed my children!' (1255-7; cf. 1249-50). We are reminded of 'the father-killer Oedipus who sowed the holy field of his mother where he had been nurtured and endured the bloodstained root he had sown' at *Seven* 752-6. *Oedipus the King* may well have been influenced by the Aeschylean *Oedipus* which preceded *Seven*. Exactly how is irretrievable, but *Seven* gives us further clues about Aeschylean influence on *Oedipus the King*. The opening scene of both plays is very similar, showing the leader of Thebes addressing his people, who are gathered to hear what he has to say, and subsequently leave. Also, Eteocles' notion of his name being the 'one' on the lips of all the citizens should the city fall (*Seven* 6) has been connected to Sophocles' presentation of the confusion between 'one' and 'many' which is developed in the context of Laius' mystery murderer(s) in *Oedipus the King*.[23]

This last point must remain somewhat speculative. It is easier to detect the influence of *Seven* in *Oedipus at Colonus*, a Sophoclean play more directly related to the storyline of *Seven*. The focus in Sophocles is on the sisters Antigone and Ismene, but the brothers are still important, especially Polynices who is a character in the play. The tragedy is set on the eve of the conflict between the two brothers, but Oedipus is still alive. He has arrived at Colonus with Antigone after much wandering. Towards the end of the play, Polynices comes to seek his father's support, having been told by an oracle that victory lies with whomever Oedipus joins. He has already gathered his army and is set to attack Thebes. Notably, the seven champions he lists (1313-25) are the same as those that we find in *Seven*, including Eteoclus instead of Adrastus, and Polynices refers to their oath taken at *Seven* 42-8, to take Thebes or die in the attempt (1302-7). But the great innovation on Sophocles' part is that, in this play, Oedipus curses his sons only *after* their quarrel. They have neglected the care of their father for years and Oedipus' wretched state is emphasized in the drama. He looks like a filthy beggar, dressed in rags. This is why Oedipus rejects his son's plea and responds by explicitly cursing both his sons to die at each other's hands. There is no ambiguity in the curse as in *Seven*, but it has been noted that there is a strong parallel between *Seven* 711-19 and *Oedipus at Colonus* 1414-34, where young maidens fail in their attempts to persuade one of the brothers to refrain from embarking on fratricide.[24]

Euripides' *Suppliant Women* (produced *c.* 424-420) deals with the direct aftermath of the battle between the Argive expedition and the Thebans from the point of view of the Argives rather than the Thebans. The Chorus of Argive mothers remember the 'tokens' (*mnêmata*) that their sons had sent home on the eve of battle (972-3), a reminder of the Aeschylean attackers' 'tokens' (*mnêmeia*) in *Seven* (49). The moderate characters of the attackers described in Euripides are a stark contrast to the heroes of *Seven*, possessed by Ares. It has been argued that Euripides' heroes represent different types of civic virtue, where praise for Thebes is an implicit criticism of Athenian democracy.[25] Scholars have also noted strong parallels between the female lament at *Suppliant Women* 778-836 and various choral aspects of Aeschylus' *Seven*. Perhaps most striking is the word Erinys, used as the closing word of both the third choral song (second stasimon) of *Seven* (791) and the lament in *Suppliant Women* (836).[26]

Lines 845-56 of *Suppliant Women* have been seen as an comment on the unrealistic nature of the messenger's detailed description of the attacking warriors in *Seven*. Theseus in the *Suppliant Women* claims that he will avoid the question of which antagonist met which since such things are in any case unclear in the context of war where spears are flying thick and fast. In the same vein Eteocles in *Phoenician Women* (751-2) declares that it would be a great waste of time to list each of the enemy by name when they are stationed at Thebes' very walls. These passages have been taken as criticism of the lengthy shield scene in *Seven*. But the references can be read with a certain amount of self-awareness on Euripides' part. As one editor of *Suppliant Women* notes: 'Euripides has just given his own Messenger such a speech (650-730 ...) and it is wholly in his manner to laugh at Tragic conventions he himself accepts'.[27]

Roman tragedy

All of these tragic versions had an impact on the reception of the Theban saga in Roman literature, and several provided direct inspiration for Roman tragedy. In the last decades of the second century BC, the tragedies of Accius dominated the Roman stage. He wrote several plays inspired by the Theban saga including a *Phoenician Women*. Notably, Accius seems to have been the first Roman tragedian to dramatize the civil war and fratricide at Thebes. This coincides with the political message repeated in many of his plays, warning against the overthrow of legitimate government, a reaction against the Gracchi's accession to power.[28]

The later tragedian Seneca, writing in the first century AD, also treated the civil war at Thebes under the title *Phoenician Women*, combining plot elements from *Oedipus at Colonus* and Euripides' *Phoenician Women*. A Stoic philosopher and tragic poet, Seneca was tutor to the infamous emperor Nero. Seneca's *Phoenician Women*, apparently an incomplete tragedy (just 664 lines long), is thought to have been one of Seneca's last plays, perhaps left incomplete because of his death in 65 AD, a consequence of his fall from favour with Nero. The play ends before the fratricide occurs, but tyrannical lust for power and the family incest are two prominent concerns of the play developed from previous versions. Eteocles' final words which close the play, 'Power is well established at any price', highlight a recurring Senecan concern in exploring the nature of tyranny and the tyrannical ruler. Incest is also something heavily emphasized in Seneca's *Oedipus*, leading some to speculate as to whether Seneca was making veiled reference to the unnatural designs which Nero was alleged to have had on his mother. In Seneca's *Phoenician Women*, the incest is set against the Roman values of parental and filial *pietas*, referring to the sacred relationship which should exist between parents and children. The males are characterized by *impietas*, a parallel to the overwhelming association of the male with impiety in *Seven*.

Seneca's innovation in making Jocasta intervene on the

battlefield may well have suggested itself from a parallel in the Roman tradition where Coriolanus is confronted by his mother as he marches on Rome, a scene dramatized in Shakespeare's *Coriolanus*.[29] There are other reasons why the Theban saga is relevant to Rome. Although one of the brothers survived, Rome's own foundation myth was based on a fratricide – that of Remus by Romulus – and the first century BC had seen a string of civil wars in Rome which would later be presented as *cognates acies* 'war between kin' in Lucan's epic *Pharsalia*. In such a climate of civil war, the dramatization of a fratricidal war was bound to resonate with contemporary sensitivities.[30]

Ancient epic

The Theban saga was an important part of the epic cycle which pre-dated *Seven* and contained two relevant epics, the *Oedipodeia* and the *Thebaid*, known to us by name and a few fragments. It has been argued that making Oedipus' children a product of his incest was Aeschylus' invention. In previous versions, it seems, Oedipus' children were the product of a second marriage after the discovery and dissolution of his first incestuous union.[31] We know of a further lost *Thebaid*, an epic poem written by Antimachus of Colophon on the subject of the expedition of the Seven against Thebes. Dating to the late fifth or early fourth century, this epic was probably written in twenty-four books, and is likely to have been influenced by *Seven* in some of its aspects. Antimachus' narrative elegy *Lyde* contains a very broad range of references to different mythological events, suggesting that he had a wide knowledge of earlier poetry which he referred to in his own work. In terms of his reputation, Antimachus seems to have provoked an extreme reaction of either admiration or disgust. The young Plato was a great fan of Antimachus' poetry, which was said to have had a strong moral and educational tone. Otherwise he appears to have been unpopular. Hellenistic poets were also divided. Antimachus was much admired by Apollonius Rhodius and greatly despised by Callimachus.[32]

Another epic poet whose work has been both admired and despised during the course of its reception history is Statius, whose twelve-book epic *Thebaid* does, in fact, survive.[33] Written in the late first century AD, this is the only surviving ancient epic which treats the Theban saga. There are story-patterns clearly inspired by the *Phoenician Women* plays – the *teichoskopia*, Oedipus' imprisonment at Thebes, the death of Menoeceus, Jocasta's intervention on the battlefield; and the summoning of the ghost of Laius recalls Seneca's *Oedipus*.[34] The clearest development of a theme important in *Seven* is the personification of Oedipus' curse as a single Fury, called Tisiphone. She is summoned by Oedipus in Book 1 and is ultimately responsible for orchestrating the fratricide in Book 11, as is illustrated in a manuscript of Statius published in France c. 1405 and held by the British Library. The brothers are represented as medieval knights, each wearing full armour and a gold crown, inflicting a mortal wound on each other simultaneously. On the left they are watched by King Adrastus and his daughter Argia, wife of Polynices. On the right, the grim Fury personified, crawling with snakes, looks on (see Fig. 5). The issue of responsibility for the fratricide is thus more straightforward than in *Seven*, but the wrath of the Fury is taken to arguably Roman extremes in the *Thebaid*,[35] when she drives the dying Tydeus to gnaw at the flesh of Melanippus' head in glee at the end of Book 8.[36]

Early Christian writers

Although the myth of the Seven was not one of the most common pagan myths engaged with by early Christian writers, it has been argued that, where it does appear, the myth is used for a different range of rhetorical purposes. For both Orosius and Clement of Alexandria, the war was a significant point in a universal chronology. Others, such as Origen and Eusebius of Caesarea, used the myth to explore concepts of free will and fate.[37] A work attributed to Fulgentius the Mythographer (late

Fig. 5. 'Eteocles and Polynices in Combat', illustration from a French manuscript of Statius, *c.* 1405. British Library, Burney 257.f.187v.

fifth century AD), but generally considered to date from the twelfth or thirteenth century, is *On the Thebaid* (or *Super Thebaiden*), a short commentary on the *Thebaid* myth which presents it as a moral allegory. It is quite bizarre and based on a whole series of erroneous, and in most cases ludicrous, etymologies. The Seven are the liberal arts, fated to die. Thebes is a soul full of virtues because it is alleged to be pronounced in Greek like the word meaning the goodness of God (*theosebeia*), a false claim. Eteocles is the destruction of morals (from the Greek *êthos* (meaning morals here) and *ochleô* (?) (meaning molest?), and therefore represents greed. The etymology of Polynices' name is also mistakenly taken to be 'the conqueror of many', that is, lust. Clearly Christian morality is a strong influence in this curious work.[38]

The Seven as crusaders

The earliest appearance of the story of *Seven* after the Dark Ages is the *Roman de Thèbes*, dated to the mid-twelfth century, by an unknown author. Although the author would have lacked access to Greek tragedies and used Statius as a primary source, it is nevertheless interesting to note the developments made, and the work is an important marker in the legacy of the civil war and fratricide at Thebes. Written, it is thought, for the Plantagenet court of Henry II, the work is dotted with contemporary references, such as the fact that Tydeus is presented as armed with a particular sword forged by Galanz, a figure from Germanic epic. The sword itself, described at 1672-77, is thought to have evoked a similar treasure owned by the counts of Anjou.[39] The theme of *Seven*, or the *Thebaid*, will have had a particular resonance in this period with those who remembered the bitter struggles for power which had taken place between the sons of William the Conqueror. However, the author of the *Roman* introduces the startling development that the mutual fratricide occurs because the brothers fail to recognize each other on the battle field (6208-57). This lack of recognition finds a parallel in the unwitting mutual fratricide of Balin and Balan in the Arthurian legends.

Intervention by the pagan gods of antiquity is kept to a minimum in the work. In terms of divine presence, it is rather the context of the First Crusade which is evoked. The war of siege against citadels, replicated by the siege of Monflor in the *Roman* as well as the siege of Thebes itself, creates a natural parallel with the process of Holy War. There are also direct references to the First Crusade. Amphiaraus, for example, who is archbishop, is compared to Godefroi de Bouillon, leader of the First Crusade (5184-5). Similarly Nestor, a young Argive knight, is said to be the son of the Duc de Châtillon (11351-2), a name strongly associated with war on the Infidels. The Thebans are presented as being in league with Turks and other Infidels, and Eteocles is a far more odious character than his brother, but there are good and evil in both camps. The overall atmosphere is one of inevitable war.

The *Roman de Thèbes* was the inspiration for John Lydgate's early fifteenth-century verse narrative *The Siege of Thebes, c.* 1420-2, which is written as an additional Canterbury tale with the author himself as the narrator. The work stresses the need for good government and peace, with Eteocles demonized as a deceptive and brutal king, and Polynices little more sympathetic, as an inglorious knight. Notably Tydeus is idealized in a way which some have argued suggests an identification with Henry V, a stark departure from the arrogant and fearsome Tydeus of *Seven*.[40]

Politics and religion in Early Modern Europe

There are three important French dramatic treatments of the Theban fratricidal war dating from the sixteenth and seventeenth centuries. Robert Garnier's *Antigone ou la Pieté* of 1580, Jean de Rotrou's *Antigone*, written in 1637 and published two years later, and Racine's 1664 *La Thébaïde ou les Frères ennemis*. Garnier's play is the most political. The quarrel between the brothers is presented as a parallel for conflicts between Catholics and Protestants at the time. When Jocasta advises her sons to renounce their differences and unite against Asia, it is a thinly veiled suggestion that Christians should do the same. The mythical civil war enables Garnier to issue an indirect critique of what he saw as the increasingly partisan spirit of the French, and to suggest that the wellbeing of their country could only be achieved through unity.[41] He places a much stronger emphasis on the absurdity of a prince sacking his own country than we find in the ancient sources, again a comment on the type of religious wars exemplified by the conflict between rival princes Henri III and Henri de Navarre, which took place in the same year as Garnier's production. Polynices is painted in a negative light as he insists on seizing power against the will of the Theban subjects, who fear him and prefer Eteocles.

To emphasize the excessive horror of civil war, Garnier attaches the prefix 'entre-' to many of the verbs he uses to describe violence, verbs which are already reflexive. The most relevant example, perhaps, is 's'entre-tuer', literally meaning something like 'to inter-kill each other', but there are many others.[42] This gives an extra weight to the quarrel and fratricide comparable to Aeschylus' use of the *auto-* prefix in *Seven*, discussed in Chapter 2, emphasizing reciprocity of action with a formula which has no real equivalent in English. The incest is also emphasized in Garnier, but here it is expressed as a devil's curse in a Christian context.[43]

In Rotrou, the quarrel between the brothers is presented in terms of 'cursed ambition', 'abominable plague' and 'a monster thirsty for blood' (79-80), and this motif of abomination is developed through the theme of nature and its revulsion at the crimes of the Labdacids. The graphic nature of the incest is also emphasized, as at 454-6. As regards the characterization of the brothers, Rotrou seems to follow Garnier. Some fault lies with Eteocles, but he is far more sympathetic than Polynices and has the support of his people. In spite of this, Polynices, like his Aeschylean counterpart, feels that justice is on his side (308).

In Racine's *Thébaïde*, a deeply personal drama, both brothers are thoroughly evil. In this his first tragedy, Racine is marking his rebellion from his family and upbringing.[44] He chose to reject religion and follow his love of the theatre at a time when the two were completely incompatible, the one aiming to suppress emotions, the other to liberate them. So his plays are full of passion, and his *Thébaïde* is particularly full of violent passion. There is no real concern here with the city's safety, in contrast to previous versions, and there is an overriding emphasis on blood. Blood-related words occur four times as often in this play as in Racine's other tragedies.[45] Confrontation between enemy brothers is a recurrent motif in Racine and conflict over power is a common theme in his plays.[46] His Eteocles and Polynices are characterized by their extreme hatred for each other and ultimately for themselves. Words for 'hate', 'rage', 'cruel', and 'inhuman' occur far more frequently than in Racine's other dramas.[47] Racine's rejection of religion is clear through the position of blame put on the father throughout the play. The progeny of Oedipus are victims of their father's crimes (428-30).

The play was only moderately successful and has remained one of Racine's least popular tragedies. However it lived on to inspire Jane Robe's *The Fatal Legacy: A Tragedy* which played in London in 1723, and is mentioned as a source in the publication accompanying the play: 'An Abstract of the Lives of Eteocles and Polynices: Necessary to be perused by the Spectators of the New Tragedy, called, *The Fatal Legacy*'. Polynices is presented as a tyrannical pretender to the throne. He and his army are a clear analogue to the Jacobites, supporters of the deposed King James II and his descendants, who were making repeated attempts to regain the British throne after the Revolution of 1688, most recently in 1715 and 1719, just a few years before *The Fatal Legacy* was produced. The defeat of the attackers against Thebes created a naturally strong anti-Jacobite message.[48]

Seven for modern times

After *The Fatal Legacy*, we find only obscure treatments of the Theban Saga: Friedrich Heinrich Bothe's *Der Ödipiden Fall oder Die Brüder* (1822), Ippolito Pindemonte's *Eteocle e Polynice* (1828), and a performance of *Seven* at Beloit College (Greek Department), Wisconsin USA (1888), which seems to be the first modern production of Aeschylus' *Seven*. The college produced Greek plays with decreasing regularity between 1885 and 1931. Produced twenty-three years after the end of the American civil war, it is difficult to posit that this performance of *Seven* had any contemporary political message.

The twentieth and twenty-first centuries have seen a great revival of interest in Greek tragedy across many countries, though relatively speaking *Seven* has remained unpopular, probably because it features such long choral odes and monologues with little that a modern audience would call 'action'. A search of the database of the Oxford Archive of Performances of Greek and Roman Drama lists 737 hits for productions inspired by Aeschylus' *Agamemnon*, and just 52 for *Seven*. However its appeal survives through the opportunities it affords both for commenting on civil war, and for exploring the dramatic form of tragedy. In 1924 a production of *Seven* at the dramatic festival of Syracuse, in an Italian translation by Ettore Romagnoli, met with great success, and shortly thereafter the festival 'became a useful tool in Mussolini's machine'.[49]

In the later twentieth century, Aeschylus' *Seven* was performed variously in several European countries (including Italy, Greece, France, Poland, Belgium, Germany, and Britain) and worldwide in locations including the US and Japan. Details of these productions, as known, are given in the database of the Oxford Archive of Performances of Greek and Roman Dramas.[50] It is beyond the scope of this volume to investigate each of these productions and their possible contexts but *Seven* has clearly retained an ability to deliver a powerful message, and can be engaged with on different levels, as will be illustrated by a number of case studies. The message of one Cuban adaptation of *Seven*, first produced in 1968, proved so politically contro-versial that it was banned by Castro's government, in spite of having won a prestigious drama award. Arrufat's *Los siete contra Tebas* uses the Theban myth to allegorize the 1961 Bay of Pigs attack on Cuba, when Cuban exiles supported by the American government launched an attack on Castro's forces and were thoroughly defeated. The parallel ends, of course, where Eteocles dies. Castro, the Eteocles figure, remains very much alive in Cuba after the Bay of Pigs, but the perceived failure of Eteocles' government in the play was interpreted as a criticism of Castro's régime.

It was only in 2001, over thirty years after the play's original production, that the play was republished with a new introduc-tion which does not, as the old one did, condemn the play, but it has never been performed in Cuba. The message of *Seven* is that victory in civil war comes at a substantial price, and this suggestion was not well received by the Cuban government. The tensions between *polis* and *genos* in Aeschylus are articu-lated more through the opposition of materialism vs.

communism in Arrufat. The golden weapons of the attackers fail against the old and shabby weapons of the Thebans. There is no doubt that the play supports communism, but it is the presentation of power which can be understood as controversial. Neither brother is entirely sympathetic. Each blames the other, and neither can see his own flaws. Ultimately the play condemns both aristocratic rule and absolute power.[51]

A radical interpretation of a different kind is to be found in Einar Schleef's *Die Mütter*, an adaptation of *Seven* combined with Euripides' *Suppliant Women*, which was performed at the Frankfurt Spielhaus in 1986, and has been discussed by Fischer-Lichte.[52] We are told that the production lasted almost four hours and was characterized by Schleef's exploitation of the two Choruses (the maidens from *Seven* and the mothers from *Suppliant Women*). Although this was his only production of Greek tragedy, the Chorus became a trademark of his theatrical art. In *Die Mütter* the Choruses were used to express the tension between the individual and the community, perhaps a reflection of the *polis / genos* conflict in *Seven*, discussed in Chapter 2. The struggle between language and body is another feature of the Chorus explored by Schleef where the language of his Choruses seeks to subordinate the rhythm of their bodies and vice versa, often creating unsettling syntactical effects and even incomprehensible language. In contrast to Arrufat, Schleef is not seeking to create a political message. Rather, he is searching for the essence of tragic theatre and, strongly influenced by Nietzche's *Birth of Tragedy*, he finds the essence of true tragedy in its Chorus. In looking back to tragedy's origins to create a theatre based on the Chorus, it is not surprising that Schleef took inspiration from *Seven*, one of the earliest surviving tragedies in which, as we saw in Chapter 5, the Chorus play a highly significant role.

A similarly innovative treatment of *Seven* is Mario Martone's 1998 film *Rehearsals for War (Teatro di Guerra)*, discussed by Michelakis and Fusillo.[53] The action is set during the civil war in former Yugoslavia (in 1995), and includes footage from rehearsals for Martone's 1996 stage production of *Seven* produced by Teatri Uniti. These rehearsals are presented under the guise of a new production to be performed in Sarajevo. The project is ultimately abandoned when the director's contact in Sarajevo is killed, and the film concludes in an open-ended fashion. The abandonment of the production reflects reality's intervention in theatre, a recurring theme in Martone's work. The influence of *Seven* has also been perceived in a less obvious corner of the twentieth century: the works of the French writer Jean Vercors (1902-91). In particular his novel *Le Silence de la Mer* (1942) is shown to portray a protagonist bound by the law of 'blood and earth' (a recurring motif in all Vercors' works), who re-enacts the crimes of his forefathers.[54]

The most recent treatment of *Seven* to date, Will Power's 2006 hip-hop adaptation produced at the New York Theatre Workshop, is in stark contrast to all previous investigations of the Theban fratricide, since it was reportedly light-hearted and amusing. Inspiration may have come from the popular musical *Blood Brothers*, which has hints of events in *Seven* although the plot is substantially different. The brothers do end up dead because of each other, but the plot plays on the mistaken identities of the brothers who were separated at birth, only meeting later, and there is no siege or war in sight. Power's *Seven* has received mixed reviews, but it cannot be denied that he has made the story widely accessible for a very broad audience. The rivalry between the brothers and their war is preserved and the stage setting was said to be 'Greek-style', with 'battle scenes that [felt] mythic'. But the heroes who join Polynices to attack Thebes become superheroes of a recognizably twentieth- and twenty-first-century type. Using hip-hop, rhythm and blues, funk, blues, and gospel for the score, the production was designed for a popular market and must easily be the performance of *Seven* to reach the widest audience in recent times.[55]

Recurring themes

The themes with which *Seven* engaged in its original context can also be seen to inform subsequent treatments of the play and the myth it dramatizes. Concerns of individual vs. community, expressed as *genos* vs. *polis* in Aeschylus, continue to be important in every historical period. The attacking Thebans are crusaders fighting for a common cause, or the brothers are obsessed with individual power at the expense of their community, sometimes Eteocles (as in Euripides' *Phoenician Women*, the *Roman de Thèbes*, and Lydgate's *Siege of Thebes*), sometimes Polynices (as in Garnier, Rotrou, and Robe), and sometimes both (as in Sophocles' *Oedipus at Colonus*, Racine, and Arrufat). Issues of religion take on different meanings through the centuries. The Thebans are Infidels (the *Roman*), or Protestants (Garnier, Robe); the attackers are Christians or Catholics. But the power of the Curse also remains. Many have stressed the horror of incest as a manifestation of the family curse (Seneca, Garnier, Rotrou), and the curse becomes that of the devil in a Christian context, as in Garnier. The violence of war is emphasized by virtually all treatments of the fratricidal conflict, though few have revisited the tension between male and female in the way that Schleef did.

It has often been said in recent years, in defending the continuing relevance of Classics in the modern world, that Greek tragedy retains its appeal because it captures and investigates timeless anxieties of the human condition. Of course, there is a strong sense in which Greek tragedy is *not* timeless, particularly in terms of its performance conventions. But the medium of myth through which Greek tragedy is expressed contains two key qualities which allow each new generation, as already in antiquity, to explore its power in a newly relevant context. These qualities are, first, its malleability, which means that the same myth can be used to illustrate a huge range of viewpoints, and, second, its remove from reality through the filter of mythology, which makes the messages conveyed through tragic myth have the potential for universal appeal.

Notes

1. Play and Trilogy

1. The complete fragments from lost plays are collected in Radt's edition of the third volume of the fragments of Greek tragedy (*Tragicorum Graecorum Fragmenta*), which features Greek text with a Latin commentary. Selected fragments (edited by Hugh Lloyd-Jones) are translated in Smyth's second Aeschylus volume in the Loeb Classical Library series, soon to be replaced by Sommerstein's new editions and translations for the same series.

2. See Carter, 'Was Attic Tragedy Democratic?', 6 and 10. Other civic ceremonies conducted at the Dionysia during the course of the fifth century included the parading and glorification of war orphans, whose citizen fathers had died in battle, and the display of tribute received by Athens' allies (post 454).

3. See Carter, 'Was Attic Tragedy Democratic?', 10-13.

4. It is difficult to ascertain whether women attended the City Dionysia, but it seems possible, if not probable, that they did. See Revermann, *Comic Business*, 166-8 with bibliography at 167 n. 12.

5. This is recorded in the *didaskaliai*, i.e. official records of dramatic productions and their outcomes; printed in Radt's *Tragicorum Graecorum Fragmenta* (vol. 3) at Testimonia 58a-b.

6. The Chorus can leave and return in some rare cases where there is a change of scene, such as in Aeschylus' *Eumenides* (230-55) and Sophocles' *Ajax* (814-66). The Chorus can occasionally leave for other reasons, as in Euripides' *Alcestis* (746-861) where they take part in a funeral procession or Euripides' *Helen* (385-515) where they accompany Helen to consult the omniscient Theonoe.

7. On Aeschylean tragic trilogies, see Sommerstein, *Aeschylean Tragedy*, 53-69; on Aeschylean tetralogies (tragic trilogies and accompanying satyr play) see Gantz, 'The Aischylean Tetralogy'.

8. The fragments of *Laius* and *Oedipus* are listed with commentary in Radt's *Tragicorum Graecorum Fragmenta* (vol. 3), and are discussed in English by Sommerstein, *Aeschylus I*, in his introduction to *Seven*.

9. This is the view of most scholars, but Roisman, 'Oedipus' Curse', argues that the curse is connected with Oedipus' discovery of his incest.

10. On the *Seven* trilogy, see further Sommerstein, *Aeschylean Tragedy*, 121-8, and Conacher, *Earlier Plays*, 36-9.

11. See further the introduction to Seaford's edition of *Cyclops*.

12. For more information on *Sphinx*, see Sommerstein, *Aeschylean Tragedy*, 129-30, Simon, *Das Satyrspiel Sphinx*, and Krumeich, Pechstein, and Seidensticker, *Das griechische Satyrspiel*, 189-96.

13. Conacher, *Earlier Plays*, 39.

14. See Sommerstein, 'Violence in Greek Drama'.

15. See Taplin, *Stagecraft*, 169, on this issue.

16. See, for example, Wiles, *Tragedy in Athens*.

17. Andrisano, 'La definizione dello spazio'.

18. Whether or not there was a raised stage on which the protagonists acted, connected to the orchestra below, where the Chorus sang and danced (possibly connected by some steps), is a hotly debated issue. No theatre structures from the fifth century survive, but in *Seven*, where there is no need for a *skênê*, it is likely that there was no raised stage. Scholars who reject the idea of a raised stage include Pickard-Cambridge, *The Theatre of Dionysus*, 67-74, and, more recently, Wiles, *Tragedy in Athens*, 63-6. Others support the view that the Greek theatre employed a raised stage, such as Arnott, *Greek Scenic Conventions*, 28-40, and Taplin, *Stagecraft*, 441.

19. See further Sommerstein, *Aeschylean Tragedy*, 102-9, and Winnington-Ingram, '*Septem*', 10.

20. For further examples, see *Lexicon Iconographicum Mythologiae Classicae* under the entry 'Septem'.

21. Sommerstein, *Aeschylean Tragedy*, 132.

22. For an accessible and concise overview of the problems in the ending of *Seven*, see Sommerstein, *Aeschylean Tragedy*, 130-4. For more technical scholarly debate with extensive bibliography, see Hutchinson, *Septem*, commentary on lines 1005-78, and also Dawe 'The End of *Seven*'. Other useful discussions are Winnington-Ingram, '*Septem*', 3-4 with n. 4, and Thalmann, *Dramatic Art*, 137-41.

2. City and Family

1. The premise of Aristophanes' comedy *Frogs* is that one of the great deceased tragedians must be brought back from the Underworld so that the poet can educate the people and 'save the *polis*'. Plato famously distrusted the concept of poets as teachers. His problem with poets, as discussed in the *Republic* (595-608), is that they often portray characters with flaws. These flaws, it is argued, can be admired and imitated by the spectators. For this reason, poets will not be allowed in the ideal state. The absence of the *polis* from Aristotle's *Poetics*, a treatise on drama written in the mid-fourth century, seems to reflect the loosening of Athens' grip on tragedy as it came to be a more international art form in this period. See Hall, 'Is there a *Polis*'.

2. Greek tragedy's emphasis on the *polis* and on Athens has often been seen as intrinsically linked to democracy, see Goldhill, 'The Great Dionysia', and Goldhill, 'Civic Ideology' for this approach. However, this view has been challenged, and it has been suggested that issues seen as specific to the democratic *polis* of Athens are, in fact, more broadly applicable to Greek *poleis* generally. See Rhodes, 'Nothing To Do With Democracy' and Carter, 'Was Attic Tragedy Democratic?' Much work on the concept of the *polis* in ancient Greece has been done in the last decades by the Copenhagen *Polis* Centre, with the aim of broadening research on the *polis* as an institution and moving away from an Athenocentric approach. The most accessible work on the subject is Hansen, *Polis and City-State*, although this may still be a challenging read for the non-specialist.

3. On anachronism in Greek tragedy, see Easterling, 'Anachronism'.

4. See, in general, Podlecki, *Political Background*.

5. On the presentation of politics in this play, see Goldhill, 'Battle Narrative and Politics', Hall, *Aeschylus: Persians* 1-28, Pelling, 'Aeschylus' *Persae* and History', and Harrison, *The Emptiness of Asia*, chs 2 and 8.

6. See further Sommerstein, 'The Theatre Audience'.

7. See further Macleod, 'Politics and the *Oresteia*', and Goldhill, *Aeschylus: The Oresteia*, 1-11 and 81-4.

8. A structuralist approach to the *polis* of Thebes as presented in Greek tragedy is adopted by Zeitlin, who sees it as the 'negative model to Athens's manifest image of itself with regard to its notions of the proper management of city, society, and self', in 'Thebes: Theater of Self' 102. See also Zeitlin's *Under the Sign*, 191-219, on the development of the self in *Seven*. More recently, a broader approach to the image of the *polis* has been stressed by Easterling, 'The Image of the *Polis*'; see esp. 56-8 on the topography of the *polis* in *Seven*.

9. Winnington-Ingram, *Septem*, 43.

10. See e.g. Sommerstein, *Aeschylean Tragedy*, 115-21; Thalmann, *Dramatic Art*, 31-81.

11. Zeitlin, *Under the Sign*, 29. Conacher, *Earlier Plays*, 39-40, acknowledges the shift in focus from 'city' to 'family' in broad terms, but also stresses the symbiosis of civic and personal destinies in the play.

12. See 648, 700, 740, 877, 880, 881, 895, 915.

13. Gods are infrequently referred to in this form in other extant tragedies of Aeschylus. The only real parallel is from *Suppliant Women* where the gods generally are 'born of Zeus' at 631, though we might also compare *Persians* 643 where Darius is a 'Sousa-born god'.

14. These seem to be the main features of the myth, though some later variations in detail are recorded. See Gantz, *Early Greek Myth*, 467-73.

15. See Sommerstein, *Aeschylean Tragedy*, 97.

16. A line missing in the text of *Seven* makes it unclear what kind of mothers they were. Sommerstein, *Aeschylus I*, conjectures something meaning 'noble' which seems likely; see also Hutchinson, *Septem* on 792. In any case the relationship of the Chorus with their mothers represents a natural bond and a contrast to the relationships between mother and child in the royal house of Thebes.

17. See Faraone, 'Molten Wax', on this issue.

18. The fragments of Ephorus are available in Greek in Jacoby's edition of the fragments of the Greek historians at #70, 2A:43-109.

19. See Hutchinson, *Septem*, commentary on lines 734-41, and compare also lines 681, 805, 848-50, 916-17.

20. This view was seriously challenged some time ago by Podlecki, 'The Character of Eteocles' (see his article for bibliography on proponents of this view), but some scholars have continued to argue that Eteocles has no freedom of choice, e.g. Thalmann, *Dramatic Art*, 146-9.

21. On human choice in the *Oresteia*, see Hammond, 'Personal Freedom'. On this issue more generally in Greek tragedy, see Halliwell, 'Human Limits'.

22. Thalmann, *Dramatic Art*, 35.

23. Burnett, 'Curse and Dream', argues for the *Opfertod* theory. Against, see Podlecki, 'The Character of Eteocles', 295-9, and 'The Concept of Leadership', 65-72. Thalmann, *Dramatic Art*, 180 n. 1, rejects the theory *per se* though he agrees with the general premise of the theory that the salvation of the city rests on the death of the brothers. But this premise dates back to the oracle Laius received which had nothing to do with an *Opfertod*. Zeitlin, *Under the Sign*, 161-8, argues that Eteocles refuses to take up a sacrificial function and so rejects a position of expiatory sacrifice or *Opfertod*.

24. See Sommerstein, 'The Seniority of Polyneikes'.

25. See Cameron, *Studies on the Seven*, 14 and 56-7, and Thalmann, *Dramatic Art*, ch. 3.

26. For a treatment of allotment in the *Iliad* and *Seven*, see Demont, 'Lots héroïques'. Berman, *Myth and Culture*, 117-77 also discusses succession and allotment in detail.

3. Divine Forces and Religious Ritual

1. Parker, *Polytheism and Society*, 136. Even Scullion, 'Nothing to do with Dionysus', who makes the controversial argument that tragedy is misconceived as ritual, cannot deny that tragedy is 'deeply engaged with religious issues' and 'full of ritual' (136).

2. See Zeitlin, 'The Motif of the Corrupted Sacrifice'.

3. See Sourvinou-Inwood, *Tragedy and Athenian Religion*, 210-13, Parker, *Polytheism and Society*, 137.

4. Sourvinou-Inwood, *Tragedy and Athenian Religion*, 227-31, gives a brief overview of how *Seven* 'is concerned with, sets out and problematizes, questions which are of major religious importance' (228).

5. Scullion, 'Saviours of the Father's Hearth'.

6. Athena can be just as war-hungry as Ares, although she has many civilizing attributes; see Deacy, 'Athena and Ares'.

7. It is interesting to note that horse and wolf, associated here with Poseidon and Apollo respectively, were thought, in ancient Greece, to be personifications of the *aôroi*, spirits of those who had died too young. See Johnston, *Restless Dead*, 180-3.

8. Pfeiffer, *History of Classical Scholarship*, 46.

9. On the Greek understanding of breathing as both an internal and external causality, and how this is exploited by the poets, see Padel, *In and Out of the Mind*, 88-98. The image of destructive breath is used of the Furies by Aeschylus in his *Eumenides* at 52-3, 137-8, and 840.

10. See Lloyd-Jones, 'Artemis and Iphigenia', 87-8.

11. See Watson, *Arae*, 74, for this treatment of curses which is particular to Greek tragedy.

12. It seems unlikely that the Furies were thought of as anthropomorphic before the *Oresteia*. See Prag, *The Oresteia*, 44-51.

13. Sommerstein, *Eumenides*, commentary on 52, suggests that in *Eumenides* the Furies wore black masks.

14. See Sommerstein, *Eumenides*, 7, for references.

15. See Aeschylus, *Eumenides* 69-70, 185, 195, 350-1, 365-7, 386.

16. This is how the majority of scholars interpret these lines, though it has been suggested that the 'unweeping eyes' are those of Eteocles or of Oedipus, on which see Roisman, 'Dry Tearless Eyes'.

17. On the different versions of Oedipus' curse, see West, 'Ancestral Curses', 39-43.

18. See Padel, *Whom Gods Destroy*, 167-96 and 249-53.

19. The text speaks of the 'mindless madness that brought that bridal couple together' (756-7). This could refer either to Laius and Jocasta, or to Oedipus and Jocasta. It has been assumed that, since Oedipus was unaware that his coupling with Jocasta was unlawful, the mindlessness must refer to Laius. This is also the view of Sommerstein, *Aeschylus I*.

20. Polynices, who 'curses and prays' (633), has been seen as a parallel for Eteocles, who prays and invokes the Curse in the prologue. See Stehle, 'Prayer and Curse', 118-20.

21. Parker, *Miasma*, 137, compares the horror expressed by the Chorus of *Seven* at the fratricide to the treatment of fratricide in Plato's *Laws*. Interestingly, Plato finds that fratricide which occurs during civil strife *can* be expiated, by three years in exile and dissolution from the family. However, the situation in *Seven*, with the inherited ancestral curse, is very different, and as we noted in Chapter 2, the brothers in *Seven* exist in a symbiosis and their deaths are simultaneous leaving neither brother alive to seek purification.

22. Imagery of blood and curse is a similarly strong motif in Aeschylus' later *Oresteia* trilogy. See, for example, *Agamemnon* 1309, 1428, *Libation Bearers* 400-2, 840, *Eumenides* 41-2, 247, 253, 365, and see also Lebeck, *The Oresteia*, 80-91, on images of pouring and flowing which consolidate the motif of dripping blood. See also Fowler, 'Creatures of Blood', on the connection between blood and curse.

23. So Fraenkel, *Agamemnon*, commentary on line 160.

24. See Siewert, 'The Ephebic Oath', especially 107 on Aeschylus' *Persians*.

25. For further information on *ephebes*, see Vidal-Naquet, *The Black Hunter*, 106-22.

26. Aloni, 'La colpa di Eteocle', 95-100.

27. See van Wees, 'The Oath of the Sworn Bands', 136-40.

28. See e.g. Demosthenes, *Against Aristocrates* 67-8, and Antiphon, *On the Murder of Herodas* 11-15 and 88. Several examples of oaths, where the touching of sacrificial victims was required as a sanctifying feature, are discussed by Faraone, 'Molten Wax', 65-72.

29. See Guidorizzi, 'Uno scudo', 65, 67-8.

30. Quotation taken from Sourvinou-Inwood, *Tragedy and Athenian Religion*, 228. Scholars with similar views include Jackson, 'The Argument', 290-1, Hubbard, 'Tragic Preludes', 105, Conacher, *Earlier Plays*, 42-7, Sommerstein, *Aeschylean Tragedy* 111-12. Zeitlin, *Under the Sign*, 145, sees the women of the *parodos* as symbolic Furies, but also finds Eteocles an extreme and unacceptable example of male behaviour in 'Patterns of Gender', 103. More sympathetic analyses of the Chorus' position include Gagarin, *Aeschylean Drama*, 151-62, who sees their position as perfectly valid. Podlecki, 'The Concept of Leadership', 64-72, is very critical of Eteocles. Foley, *Female Acts*, 45-9, stresses the differences between male and female functions. Valakas, 'The First Stasimon', sees the role of the Chorus as creating a tension between the mythology and the reality of war.

31. Stehle, 'Prayer and Curse'. An even more recent treatment of prayer in *Seven*, Giordano-Zecharya, 'Ritual Appropriateness', apparently unaware of Stehle, is less convincing, as she fails to notice the disturbing effect of Eteocles' invocation of the Curse.

32. See e.g. Henrichs, 'Anonymity and Polarity'.

33. Noted by Hutchinson, *Septem*, on line 69.

34. Cf. Stehle, 'Prayer and Curse', 113, who analyses Eteocles' language here as 'the language of curses'.

35. See Stehle, 'Prayer and Curse', 115-16, with further bibliography.

36. On the name Eumenides, see Sommerstein, *Aeschylus: Eumenides*, 11-12. On the name of the Black Sea see Allen, 'The Name of the Black Sea'.

37. On reciprocity in Greek religion, see Seaford, *Reciprocity and Ritual*, and Pulleyn, *Prayer in Greek Religion*, 16-38.

38. The text at 278 is corrupted, but the sense seems clear enough.

39. This type of prayer *da quia dedi* 'give because I have given', reminding the god of previous worship, is a formula apparently culturally specific to Greece and appears several times in Homer. See further Pulleyn, *Prayer in Greek Religion*, 16-38. Giordano-Zecharya, 'Ritual Appropriateness', refers briefly to this passage, 65 n. 48, but suggests that it is expressed in a supplicatory tone, implying that the prayer is not properly reciprocal. She is right to emphasize the gendered approach to ritual demonstrated by Eteocles and the Chorus, but her attempts to stress choral supplication in opposition to a reciprocal male attitude to prayer are strained.

40. On the triadic structure of *Seven* in comparison to the *Oresteia*, see Zeitlin, *Under the Sign*, 16-17. On triads in the *Oresteia*, see Burian, 'Zeus Sôtêr Tritos'.

41. See Zeitlin, *Under the Sign*, 55-153, with a summary of possible schemas at 174-6.

42. See Stehle, 'Prayer and Curse', 103-5, quotation from 105.

43. See Hutchinson, *Septem*, with commentary on lines 720-91.

44. Pausanias 2.20.5, and see Podlecki, *Political Background*, 37-8.

45. Burkert, 'Seven Against Thebes', 42.

46. See Chiarini, 'Il ritorno della Sfinge'.

47. See West, 'The Midnight Planet'.

48. See Sommerstein, *Aeschylus I*, on line 802.

49. See further Brown, 'Odysseus and Polyphemus'.

50. That Eteocles anticipates being cursed is also suggested by Hubbard, 'Tragic Preludes', though he argues in terms of the vocabulary of lament and its connection with cursing.

51. The second part of Parthenopaeus' name has been connected with the Greek word for child *'pais'*. This is not etymologically sound, but Parthenopaeus is certainly called 'a man-child' (533).

52. The text here is suspected of interpolation, but the sentiment expressed follows a pattern evident in the rest of the play.

53. See Zeitlin, *Under the Sign*, 141.

54. Again, the text here is corrupt, but the meaning seems clear enough.

55. See Parker, *Polytheism and Society*, 90, on assembly consultation of oracles and procedure.

56. See Parker, *Polytheism and Society*, 118 with n. 10.

57. The end of Aeschylus' *Eumenides*, for example, provides an aetiology for the foundation of the Areopagus homicide court in Athens, and the plays of Euripides contain many aetiologies for the foundations of cults.

58. Atossa relates her dream of the metaphorical struggle between Greece and Asia at *Persians* 181-99, the Chorus speak of dreams in *Suppliant Women* (885-97), Menelaus dreams of Helen at *Agamemnon* 420-6, Clytemnestra dreams that she has given birth to a snake at *Libation Bearers* 527-35, and is herself the apparition of the Furies' dream at the opening of *Eumenides*. Io also refers to her dreams in *Prometheus Bound* 645-55.

59. Manton, 'The Second Stasimon', 79.

60. On the concept of divine and human agency as both being important elements in causation, see further DeVito, 'Eteocles, Amphiaraus, and Necessity', with further bibliography, Kirkwood, 'Eteocles Oiakostrophos', and Lesky, 'Eteocles in den Sieben' and 'Decision and Responsibility'.

4. Warriors

1. Aeschylus' own *Persians* is a good example of this phenomenon, as is, of course, Herodotus' account of the Persian wars in his *Histories*; on practicalities of Greek warfare during the Persian wars, see van Wees, *Greek Warfare*, 177-94, 241-3.

2. Scholars often find Homer's descriptions of the use of chariots unrealistic (see e.g. Rutherford, *Homer*, 38) but Homer's reliability has been defended by van Wees, *Greek Warfare*, 158-60.

3. See further van Wees, *Status Warriors*, 183-90.

4. See van Wees, *Status Warriors*, 256-7.

5. Van Wees, *Status Warriors*, 189, is controversial in suggesting that desire for booty is '[c]onspicuously absent' from the motives of the Greeks in attacking Troy; see e.g. Rutherford, *Homer*, 39.

6. The term 'shame-culture' was first used by Dodds, *The Greeks*, to describe Homeric society, see 17-18, 28, 47-50; cf. Adkins, *Merit and Responsibility*, 48-9. For a more recent treatment, see Cairns, *Aidôs*.

7. On this mark of dishonour against Achilles, see Cairns, 'Affronts and Quarrels', 211-15.

8. The term is an extremely complex one and cannot be well translated by a single English term. The most detailed study of *hybris* is Fisher, *Hybris*; see also Cairns, '*Hybris*, Dishonour'.

9. Especially in *Iliad* 9, discussed by van Wees, *Status Warriors*, 131-5, with further examples.

10. For more examples, consult the *Lexicon Iconographicum Mythologiae Classicae* under the entry 'Eteocles'.

11. Though scholars continue to engage with Adkins' work; see especially Adkins, *Merit and Responsibility*, and 'Homeric Values'. Cairns, 'Affronts and Quarrels', 203 n. 1, summarizes scholarly work which opposes and engages with Adkins' theories.

12. Van Wees, 'Heroes, Knights and Nutters', 58.

13. On sacrifice and divination before war in ancient Greece, see Parker, 'Sacrifice and Battle'.

14. See also the sinister compounds at 699, 737, 857.

15. Compare Sophocles' *Antigone* 106-9 and Euripides' *Phoenician Women* 1099, both of which describe the army attacking Thebes as 'white-shielded'.

16. Bernadete, 'Two Notes' (Part 1) argues that Eteocles' interpretation of the shield symbols becomes progressively more successful as the scene unfolds. Cameron, 'The Power of Words' focuses on Eteocles' use of language in attempting to avert the threat of the shield symbols. Judet de la Combe, 'Étéocle Interprète', also emphasizes the importance of the hermeneutics of Eteocles' responses in the shield scene.

17. Steiner, *The Tyrant's Writ*, 49-60, analyses the shield symbols as forms of communication. Zeitlin, *Under the Sign*, is also much concerned with semiotics.

18. Zeitlin, *Under the Sign*, quotation from 191; the uninitiated may find parts of this study difficult to digest.

19. Imagery is especially important for Thalmann, *Dramatic Art*; he discusses the shield scene in particular in ch. 5 (105-35).

20. See Eupolis fragment 394 (Kassel-Austin *Poetae Comici Graeci*, vol. 5), and Theopompus fragment 402 (Jacoby, *Fragmente der griechischen Historiker* 115). On shield symbols in the Greek world see further Berman, *Myth and Culture*, 33-86, esp. 58-61.

21. Referred to by Lazenby, *The Spartan Army*, 30.

22. See Taplin, 'The Shield of Achilles', 1-2.

23. Taplin, 'The Shield of Achilles'.

24. See Podlecki, *Political Background*, 30 with further bibliography, and also Rosenbloom, 'Shouting "Fire" in a Crowded Theater', 188-90.

25. See Deacy, 'Athena and Ares', 286-7.

26. See Padel, *Whom Gods Destroy*, 65-96.

27. The oath is reported by the fourth century mythographer Asclepiades (Jacoby #12), but it is clear from *Seven* 568ff. that Amphiaraus is an unwilling participant in the expedition. The bribing of Eriphyle is mentioned already in the *Odyssey* (15.247).

28. See Podlecki, *Political Background*, 37-40.

29. See Roisman, 'The Messenger and Eteocles', 30.

30. Cameron, *Studies on the Seven*, 74-84, discusses horse imagery in *Seven*, and sees it as essentially connected to the nautical imagery.

31. I cannot agree with Roisman, 'The Messenger and Eteocles', 24-5 and 33, who supposes that the shields of Capaneus, Eteoclus, and Polynices are not to be thought of as containing inscribed messages.

32. See further Easterling, 'Anachronism'; the bibliography on issues of literacy and orality in Greek culture is extensive. A good starting point is Thomas, *Literacy and Orality*.

33. On the power of the eyes in Greek religion see Vernant, *La Mort dans les Yeux*.

34. On eye-cups, see Clark, Elston, and Hart, *Understanding Greek Vases*, 90-1, Boardman, *Athenian Black Figure Vases*, 107-8, and especially Ferrari, 'Eye-Cups'.

35. See Lissarrague, *Aesthetics of the Greek Banquet*, 142.

36. Bacon, 'The Shield of Eteocles', 33.

37. It has been noticed by Burnett, 'Curse and Dream', n. 17, that the image of the Theban hand develops to become destructive when Eteocles' and Polynices' hands are armed with the fateful iron.

38. A good example of this contrast is Sophocles' *Electra* where men are associated with the sphere of action and women with the sphere of speech.

39. See, in general, Hall, *Inventing the Barbarian*.

40. Rosenbloom, 'Shouting "Fire" in a Crowded Theater', 188-90, sees the Thebans as directly reminiscent of the Athenians during the Persian Wars.

41. Zeitlin, *Under the Sign*, 78.

42. For the view that Eteoclus is an Aeschylean invention, see Garvie, 'Aeschylus' Simple Plots', 72-3. Against this, see Hutchinson, *Septem*, commentary on 457-85. The identity of the Seven changes variously through the subsequent treatments of the myth, which can be explained by shifting alliances between the Greek states and a wish to present genealogies in particular ways. For a detailed analysis of such shifts and the reasons behind them, see Cingano, 'I nomi dei Sette a Tebe'.

43. Edmunds, 'Sounds Off Stage', 108, puts forward a plausible argument suggesting that the noise of horses was intended to be heard off stage.

44. See Hall, *Persians*, 21-2.

45. See *Persians* 3, 9, 45, 53, 79, 159.

46. Golden, 'Eteocles and the Meaning of the *Septem*'.

5. Women

1. The bibliography on female presences in Greek tragedy is vast. An excellent starting point, with extensive bibliography is Foley, *Female Acts*.

2. See Zeitlin, 'Patterns of Gender'.

3. Scholars who feel Eteocles is justified in his treatment of the Chorus include: Cameron, 'The Power of Words', Jackson, 'The Argument', 290-1, Hubbard, 'Tragic Preludes', 105, Conacher, *Earlier Plays*, 42-7, Sommerstein, *Aeschylean Tragedy* 111-12, Sourvinou-Inwood, *Tragedy and Athenian Religion*, 228.

Scholars who find Eteocles excessive include Gagarin, *Aeschylean Drama*, 151-62, Zeitlin, 'Patterns of Gender', 103, Podlecki, 'The Concept of Leadership', 64-72, Stehle, 'Prayer and Curse'.

4. On the different roles of the Chorus undertaken in *Seven*, including their presence as both a collective character and a functioning Chorus, see Zimmermann, 'Coro e azione'.

5. No one, as far as I am aware, has followed Delcourt's untenable argument in 'Le Rôle du Choeur', that the Chorus are really a composite of elderly female leaders, who sing, attended by a group of subsidiary girls.

6. See Dowden, *Death and the Maiden*, 44.

7. Byrne, 'Fear in the *Seven*', argues that choral fear of rape in *Seven* is also essentially a fear of marriage. But rape and marriage are not the same (in antiquity or now), and the arguments Byrne adduces to justify her claim are unconvincing. Byrne also argues, equally unconvincingly, that Eteocles and the warriors are feminized in various ways.

8. See Brown, 'Eteocles and the Chorus'.

9. Zeitlin, 'Patterns of Gender', 103-4.

10. The structuralist and Freudian analysis of Caldwell, 'The Misogyny of Eteocles', is unconvincing. He argues, among other things, that the life of Polynices mirrors that of Oedipus, and that of Eteocles mirrors the life of Laius, and attempts to explain Eteocles' misogyny as a parallel to Laius' alleged homosexuality in his rape of the boy Chrysippus, and his rejection of Jocasta's bed in response to the oracle (214). But the term 'homosexuality' cannot be used loosely for the ancient world and pederasty did not exclude a man from married life in ancient Greece (on the complexity of issues of homosexuality in antiquity, see the introduction of Hubbard, *Homosexuality*). In any case, Laius *did not* ultimately reject Jocasta's bed, and is not an appropriate parallel for Eteocles' rejection of the entire female race.

11. This is noted by Bernadete, 'Two Notes' (Part 1), 29.

12. See Sommerstein, *Aeschylus I*, and Hutchinson, *Septem*, at the appropriate passage.

13. Other scholars have compared *Seven* with *Iliad* 6 and give alternative analyses. Foley, *Female Acts*, 47-8, argues that the behaviour of the women in *Iliad* 6 would be regarded as ill-omened by *Seven*'s Eteocles. Ieranò, 'La città delle donne', finds the women of *Seven* to be a parody of their Iliadic counterparts.

14. See Parker, *Miasma*, 194 and n. 20, and Rosivach, 'Execution by Stoning'.

15. Herodotus 3.80-2 highlights Greek perceptions of the characteristics of tyrants; on Creon's tyrannical qualities in *Antigone*, see Griffith, *Antigone*, 3, 33, 54-8.

16. Delcourt, 'Le Rôle du Choeur'.

17. McClure, *Spoken Like a Woman*, 45-6.

18. See Edmunds, 'Sounds Off Stage', 105-8.

19. See Holst-Warhaft, *Dangerous Voices*, 1 and 133-4, and also Alexiou, *The Ritual Lament*, 83-101, on historical laments for the fall or destruction of cities, ancient to modern.

20. On the disturbing content of the lament, see also Foley, *Female Acts*, 49-53. On the use of victory language to describe disasters, see Hutchinson, *Septem*, commentary on lines 951 and 953-60.

21. Foley, *Female Acts*, 51, suggests it contained the foundation of a cult for the brothers.

22. This point is made by Roisman, 'Women's Free Speech', 97, though her broad categories of 'men' and 'women' do not allow for the complexities of identity associated with each party in *Seven*.

23. Zeitlin, 'Patterns of Gender', 111, notes that 'visionary quality in Aeschylean theater is assigned to women'.

24. Noted by Edmunds, 'Sounds Off Stage', 106.

25. See Arthur, 'The Divided World of *Iliad* VI', 32-3, for analysis of this passage.

6. The Legacy: Fifth Century BC to Twenty-First Century AD

1. Griffith, *Antigone*, 7 n. 30.

2. See Sommerstein, *Frogs*, 8 and n. 38.

3. On the date of the addition, see further Hutchinson, *Septem*, xliii.

4. On the selection of seven and later three plays by Aeschylus, see Hutchinson, *Septem*, xlvii, and Reynolds and Wilson, *Scribes and Scholars*, 53.

5. See Hutchinson, *Septem*, xlviii.

6. For a list of the manuscripts and papyri, see Hutchinson, *Septem*, liii-liv.

7. See Garland, *Surviving Greek Tragedy*, 95-118, on the translation and dissemination of Greek tragedy in the fifteenth and sixteenth centuries.

8. On productions of Greek tragedy from the sixteenth to the nineteenth centuries, see Garland, *Surviving Greek Tragedy*, 115-18, 147-61.

9. See Garland, *Surviving Greek Tragedy*, 122.

10. Fraenkel, 'Die sieben Redepaare'.

11. See Podlecki, *Political Background*, 27-41, and Post, 'Seven as Propaganda'.

12. Cameron, *Studies*, 14, 56-7, and Thalmann, *Dramatic Art*, ch. 3.

13. Lloyd, *Oxford Readings in Aeschylus*, 8-13. In addition to the scholarship discussed by Lloyd, the following may be adduced. Scholars who feel Eteocles is justified in his treatment of the Chorus: Cameron, 'The Power of Words', Jackson, 'The Argument', 290-1, Hubbard, 'Tragic Preludes', 105, Conacher, *Earlier Plays*, 42-7, Sommerstein, *Aeschylean Tragedy*, 111-12, Sourvinou-Inwood, *Tragedy and Athenian Religion*, 228; and scholars who find Eteocles excessive and sympathize with the Chorus: Gagarin, *Aeschylean Drama*, 151-62, Zeitlin, 'Patterns of Gender', 103, Podlecki, 'The Concept of Leadership', 64-72, Stehle, 'Prayer and Curse'.

14. Lesky, 'Eteocles in den Sieben' and 'Decision and Responsibility', and see also Kirkwood, 'Eteocles Oiakostrophos'; Solmsen, 'The Erinys'. Of more recent scholars, Thalmann, *Dramatic Art*, 146-9, apparently still sees Eteocles as swept along by his fate. DeVito, 'Eteocles, Amphiaraus and Necessity' argues that both Eteocles and Amphiaraus share the conviction that fate is inescapable.

15. See also Lloyd, *Oxford Readings in Aeschylus*, 8-13, on the 'sacrifice' (*Opfertod*) theory in the earlier German scholarship, which Burnett, 'Curse and Dream', revives. This had already been rejected by Podlecki, 'The Character of Eteocles', 295-9, as in his later 'The Concept of Leadership', 65-72.

16. On the reception history of Medea, see Griffiths, *Medea*, Allan, *Medea*, ch. 5 (in this series), and the collection of essays in Hall, Macintosh, and Taplin, *Medea in Performance*.

17. On the lion-skin shield and on Tydeus as the figure holding the torch, see Mastronarde, *Phoenissae*, commentary on 1120-2.

18. The best known example of Euripides' direct engagement with Aeschylus is the recognition scene of his *Electra* which has been seen as a parody of the equivalent scene in Aeschylus' *Libation Bearers*; see e.g. Bond, 'Euripides' Parody of Aeschylus'.

19. On the authenticity of these lines, see Mastronarde, *Phoenissae*, commentary on lines 1104-40. For a detailed treatment of the shield scene in *Phoenician Women*, see Morin, 'La Séquence des Boucliers', who reads the shield emblems in terms of mythological history and political implications.

20. See Mastronarde, *Phoenissae*, commentary on 350, for discussion of the image of iron in both plays.

21. For a list of Euripidean and tragic exploitations of onomastic etymologies, see Platnauer, *Iphigenia in Tauris*, commentary on line 32. On Euripidean interest in names, see Wright, *Euripides' Escape Tragedies*, 149-50, 290-5, 310-16.

22. For more details on Aeschylean echoes in *Antigone*, see Griffith, *Antigone*, with commentary on relevant lines.

23. See Zeitlin, 'Theater of the Self', 111-12.

24. Noted by Long, 'Pro and Contra Fratricide', 186.

25. Besso, 'I Sette e i nuovi valori eroici'.

26. Zuntz, *Political Plays*, 11, discusses all these parallels.

27. Collard, *Supplices*, commentary on lines 846-56; see also Mastronarde, *Phoenissae*, commentary on lines 751-2.

28. See Boyle, *Roman Tragedy*, 126-7.

29. For a detailed discussion of the figure of Jocasta in this play, see Mazzoli, 'Giocasta in prima linea'.

30. For more information on Senecan and Roman drama, see Boyle, *Roman Tragedy*.

31. See Mastronarde, *Phoenician Women*, 20-2, with further bibliography.

32. See Pfeiffer, *History of Classical Scholarship*, 93-5.

33. Statius was popular in the Middle Ages, but in more recent centuries his work has been seen as inferior to other ancient epic poets, and he has only in the last few decades been treated seriously by classical scholars as a sophisticated poet.

34. On the relationship between Statius' *Thebaid* and Seneca's *Oedipus*, see Aricò, '*Crudelis vincit pater*', 169-76.

35. The plays of the Roman tragedian Seneca are often gruesome.

36. For more information on the *Thebaid*, see Vessey, *Statius and the 'Thebaid'*.

37. See further Bona, 'I Sette negli autori cristiani antichi'.

38. For more information, see Whitbread, *Fulgentius*, and Manca, '*Frangenda est littera*'.

39. See Mora-Lebrun, *Le Roman de Thèbes*, 7.

40. See Edwards, *John Lydgate*, 7.

41. Beaudin, *Antigone*, 9.

42. See Beaudin, *Antigone*, 10.

43. See Beaudin, *Antigone*, 18-23; Garnier's *Antigone* also investigates incestuous erotic desire between Antigone and Polynices, discussed by Steiner, *Antigones*, 160-2.

44. Orphaned at the age of four, Racine was given a strictly religious education by his grandparents and aunt, who was Abbess of Port-Royal. Letters from his aunt reveal that she was appalled and outraged to hear that he had been keeping company with infamous theatre types like Molière. She begs him to 'seriously consider what kind of abyss he has thrown himself into'; see Rohou, *Racine*, ii.

45. Rohou, *Racine*, 858.

46. Clashes between brothers in Racine's plays include Nero and Britannicus in *Britannicus*, Amurat, and Bajazet in *Bajazet*, Pharnace and Xipharès in *Mithridate*.

47. Rohou, *Racine*, 858.

48. The text of the play and the 'Abstract' are available to download from the Eighteenth Century Collections Online (http://galenet.gale-group.com/servlet/ECCO). The play is briefly discussed by Hall and Macintosh in *Greek Tragedy and the British Theatre*, 44, 66, 82-3.

49. Macintosh, 'Tragedy in Performance', 306.

50. For details, consult the database of the Oxford Archive for the Performances of Greek and Roman Dramas at http://www.apgrd.ox.ac.uk/database.htm.

51. For more information on this play and its relationship with Aeschylus' *Seven*, see Torrance, 'Brothers at War'.

52. Fischer-Lichte, 'Origins of Theatre', 355-9.

53. Michelakis, 'Greek Tragedy in Cinema', 205-6, and Fusillo, 'I Sette'.

54. See Fornaro, 'Polinice, von Ebrennac e il castigo del silenzio'.

55. On this production, see Frank, 'In New York', 53.

Guide to Further Reading

This guide is designed to draw attention to some key works of secondary scholarship which will provide a starting point for further reading on the central issues discussed in each chapter, as well providing guidance on texts and commentaries. Further reading on more specific issues dealt with in this Companion will be found in the relevant notes accompanying each chapter. Full bibliographical details for all works referred to can be found in the Bibliography.

General guides to Greek tragedy

Csapo and Slater, *The Context of Ancient Drama*, is a detailed sourcebook, using different kinds of evidence to construct a comprehensive guide to the context in which drama was performed in the Greek and Roman worlds.

Easterling, *Cambridge Companion to Greek Tragedy*, is an edited collection of very useful essays treating different aspects of Greek tragedy in three broad sections: historical context, dramatic context, and reception.

Goldhill, *Reading Greek Tragedy*, is a good introduction to several aspects of Greek tragedy, though *Seven* is not one of his case studies.

Gregory, *Companion to Greek Tragedy*, is an edited collection of essays, and is the most recent and comprehensive guide to Greek tragedy. It is divided into four broad sections dealing with historical and sociological context, elements of dramatic structure and production, approaches to the three great trage-dians, and issues central to Greek tragedy (including a chapter on Aeschylus, 215-32), and reception.

Sommerstein, *Greek Drama*, is a concise introduction to

dramatic genres, including tragedy (15-22), and dramatic authors, including Aeschylus (33-40), with an anthology of texts, including an excerpt from *Seven* (94-5).

Storey and Allan, *Guide to Ancient Greek Drama*, is a wide-ranging introduction to dramatic context (1-71) and different dramatic genres, including tragedy and Aeschylus (93-111), although *Seven* does not feature very prominently here.

Taplin, *Greek Tragedy in Action*, is an extremely useful introduction to performance aspects of Greek tragedy, though, again, *Seven* is not a central focus for discussion.

Seven: translations and commentaries

Dawson, *The Seven Against Thebes*. This translation and commentary is very clear, useful, and accessible. Unfortunately, however, this work is out of print.

Grene and Lattimore, *Aeschylus II*, is a good translation with line numbers corresponding to the Greek text.

Hecht and Bacon, *Aeschylus: Seven Against Thebes*, is a translation that combines the style of a poet with the understanding of a classical scholar. The effect is powerful but the line numbering does not correspond to the standard Greek text, which is unfortunate.

Hutchinson, *Aeschylus: Septem*. This is the most useful current edition of the Greek text with substantial introduction and commentary. Those unfamiliar with Greek will find it difficult to use, however.

Lupaş and Petre, *Commentaire aux Sept*. Requires knowledge of French and Greek.

Rose, *Commentary on Aeschylus*, writes on *Seven* in volume I, 162-246, but this will only be useful for those with knowledge of Greek.

Smyth, *Aeschylus I*, is an outdated and archaic translation with facing Greek, which will soon be replaced by Sommerstein, *Aeschylus I* (below).

Sommerstein, *Aeschylus I*, is an edition of Aeschylus' plays with Greek text and facing translation due, at the time of writing, to be published relatively soon. This particularly faithful translation is the recommended accompaniment to this volume. These translations will subsequently be republished for the widely accessible Penguin Classics series.

Vellacott, *Aeschylus: Prometheus Bound and Other Plays*, is at the time of writing the most widely accessible translation, though it is not as reliable as Dawson's (above). We look forward to the new Penguin translations by Sommerstein (above).

Verrall, *The Seven Against Thebes*, contains an introduction, and Greek text with simultaneous commentary followed by a translation. This translation is not recommended and the work is somewhat outdated in terms of the literary analysis of the play.

Seven in general works on Aeschylus

Conacher, *The Earlier Plays*, discusses *Seven* at 36-74 and is a useful introduction for further study of the play.

Gagarin, *Aeschylean Drama*, focuses primarily on the *Persians* and the *Oresteia*, but chapter 5 deals with the other three plays and there is a useful appendix on the relationship between Eteocles and the Chorus in *Seven*.

Herington, *Aeschylus*, 78-93, gives a general and concise overview of *Seven*.

Lloyd, *Oxford Readings in Aeschylus*, contains an essay on 'The character of Eteocles in Aeschylus' *Seven Against Thebes*' (141-73), which is particularly useful since it is a translation of a chapter from von Fritz's *Antike und moderne Tragödie* (193-226).

Podlecki, *Political Background*, deals with possible political references in *Seven* at 27-41 and remains a central study of this topic.

Rosenmeyer, *The Art of Aeschylus*, is a thematic study of Aeschylean drama. Discussion of *Seven* in particular can be found through the references in the index of passages.

Smyth, *Aeschylean Tragedy*, devotes 123-50 to *Seven* but expresses many views which are outdated.

Sommerstein, *Aeschylean Tragedy*, is the most recent and

comprehensive guide to Aeschylean tragedy. See especially 97-134 on *Seven*.

Taplin, *Stagecraft*, is a detailed scholarly treatment of Aeschylean stagecraft. *Seven* is discussed at 129-91, but this treatment is aimed at a specialist audience and may be a difficult read for the uninitiated.

Winnington-Ingram, *Studies in Aeschylus*, contains (16-54) his 1977 article '*Septem*' unchanged except for a few references to more recent bibliography. The article rather than the book has been referred to throughout this Companion. This remains an excellent starting point for studying *Seven*.

Book-length studies devoted to *Seven*

Aloni, Berardi, Besso, and Cecchin (editors), *I Sette a Tebe*, is a collection of essays which covers the impact of the myth of *Seven* from antiquity to the twentieth century. It contains one contribution in English, Edmunds, 'Sounds Off Stage', but all other essays are in Italian. A useful review of its contents, in English, by N.W. Bernstein, can be found in the electronic journal *Bryn Mawr Classical Review* at http://ccat.sas.upenn.edu/bmcr/2003/2003-12-05.html.

Berman, *Myth and Culture* is the most recent treatment of *Seven* and is a study of the play as cultural discourse, focusing on shield decoration, the topography of Thebes, issues of inheritance, and the custom of sortition. Unfortunately it was published too late for full consideration here.

Cameron, *Studies on the Seven*, is a short introduction to the mythological background of *Seven* followed by several studies on imagery in the play, especially allotment imagery, nautical imagery, horse imagery, and imagery of earth. This last is a reprint of his earlier article 'Debt to Earth'. Unfortunately this book is out of print and difficult to find outside specialist libraries.

Thalmann, *Dramatic Art*, is a useful study of *Seven*, which discusses issues of city and family in particular through various systems of imagery, as well as several structural elements in the play. Unfortunately this book is (also) out of print and difficult to find outside specialist libraries. It should also be noted that Greek quotations are not translated.

Zeitlin, *Under the Sign*, is an important study of the play which focuses on structure and symbolism in *Seven*. It contains many nuanced readings and is marked by Zeitlin's application of structuralist theory to the study of Greek tragedy. Unfortunately this book is (again) out of print and difficult to find outside specialist libraries.

1. Play and Trilogy

General material
Probably the most accessible comprehensive guide to the context of ancient drama is Storey and Allan, *Guide to Ancient Greek Drama* (1-71), but see also other works referred to under General Guides to Greek Tragedy.

Material specific to Seven
On reconstructing the trilogy of *Seven*, see Sommerstein, *Aeschylean Tragedy*, 121-30, and Conacher, *Earlier Plays*, 36-9.

On myths associated with Thebes, see Gantz, *Early Greek Myth*, 467-530.

2. City and Family

General material
On the importance of *polis* ideology for Greek tragedy, see Goldhill, *Reading Greek Tragedy*, chapter 3. Goldhill, 'The Great Dionysia', sees Greek tragedy as essentially a construct of Greek democracy, but this view has recently been challenged by Rhodes, 'Nothing to do with Democracy?', and Carter, 'Was Athenian Tragedy Democratic?' It should be noted in this context that *polis* ideology need not be democratic.

Material specific to Seven
Issues of city and family are given considerable space in Thalmann, *Dramatic Art*, chapters 2 and 3. Sommerstein,

Aeschylean Tragedy, also deals directly with this issue (115-21), as does Zeitlin, *Under the Sign* (23-36).

Political aspects of *Seven* are dealt with comprehensively by Podlecki, *Political Background*, chapter 3.

3. Divine Forces and Religious Ritual

General material:

On tragedy and religion, see Sourvinou-Inwood, *Tragedy and Athenian Religion*, whose thesis is in part a reaction against Mikalson, *Honour Thy Gods*, who engages with the same issue. Mikalson argued that the gods of tragedy are not identifiable with those of *polis* religion. Sourvinou-Inwood takes the opposite view.

On Greek religion generally, with a very useful breakdown of sections dealing with each god and ritual type separately, see Burkert, *Greek Religion*. More specifically on Athenian religion, see Parker, *Polytheism and Society*, with 136-52 dedicated to religion in the theatre.

Watson's *Arai* is a very broad-ranging survey of curses in antiquity. It does not contain much that deals specifically with Greek tragedy but is useful for gaining a broader picture of the workings of curses in antiquity.

Material specific to Seven

For those unfamiliar with Greek religious and social values, Adkins, 'Divine and Human Values', will be a useful introduction to their significance and exploitation in *Seven*.

The best treatment of prayer and curse in *Seven* is Stehle, 'Prayer and Curse'. Giordano-Zecharya, 'Ritual Appropriateness', is slightly more recent but not so convincing. The arguments of Solmsen, 'The Erinys', who suggests that the Curse takes over completely leaving the mortal protagonists as helpless victims, have long been refuted. I look forward to Sewell-Rutter, *Guilt by Descent* (forthcoming), which will discuss 'issues of inherited guilt, curses, and divine causation ... with particular reference to Aeschylus' *Seven Against Thebes* and the *Phoenician Women of Euripides*' (quoted from http://www.oup.com/uk/catalogue/?ci=9780199227334).

4. Warriors

General material
For an analysis of the male hero in early Greek poetry, see Nagy, *Best of the Achaeans*.

On ancient Greece as a warrior society, see Pritchett, *The Greek State at War*, in five volumes, and works by van Wees: *Status Warriors* and *Greek Warfare*.

Material specific to Seven
The Shield Scene is discussed by several scholars. Most detailed is Zeitlin, *Under the Sign*. Berman, *Myth and Culture*, chapter 2, discusses the shield blazons in the context of shield decoration in ancient Greece. Thalmann, *Dramatic Art*, devotes chapter 5 to the shield scene (105-35), discussing its structure, themes, and dramatic presentation. Bernadete, 'Two Notes' (Part 1), concentrates on Eteocles' interpretation of the shields, arguing for a progressive rate of success. Cameron, 'The Power of Words', highlights the way in which Eteocles exploits language in an attempt to avert the threat of the attackers. Bacon, 'The Shield of Eteocles', discusses the shields of the attackers to contextualize her thesis that the Dikê of Polynices' shield is met by the force of the Erinys with Eteocles. Vidal-Naquet, 'The Shields of the Heroes', treats of the shields as if in a pediment formation, a curious exercise. Non-English scholarship on the shield scene includes Fraenkel's *Die Sieben Redepaare*, and Judet de la Combe's 'Étéocle Interprète'.

5. Women

General material
The most detailed and recent treatment of women in tragedy is Foley, *Female Acts*, which contains an extensive bibliography. On female lament in Greek literature, see Holst-Warhaft, *Dangerous Voices*. On female speech in Greek tragedy, see McClure, *Spoken like a Woman*, and Mossman, 'Women's Voices'.

Material specific to Seven
There are few convincing treatments of the female role in
Seven, though Stehle, 'Prayer and Curse', is an excellent
starting point for the Chorus' role in prayer. See also Gagarin,
Aeschylean Drama, 151-62, on the role of the Chorus.

On female lament in *Seven*, see Foley, *Female Acts*, 45-55.

Zeitlin, 'Patterns of Gender', is another useful introduction
to gender relations in this play and in Aeschylus.

Goff, 'The Women of Thebes', building on Zeitlin's concept
of Thebes as the 'anti-Athens' (in 'Thebes: Theater of Self
and Society'), argues that Theban women are repeatedly
called to intervene in a public arena, which is not proper to
their role, and therefore makes them dangerous to the city's
welfare.

6. The Legacy: Fifth Century BC to Twenty-First
Century AD

General material
On the reception of Greek tragedy, see section 3 of Easterling,
Cambridge Companion to Greek Tragedy, and section 4 of
Gregory, *Companion to Greek Tragedy*. Other important
publications are Hall and Macintosh, *Greek Tragedy and the
British Theatre*, and the collections of essays in Hall,
Macintosh, and Wrigley, *Dionysus Since 69*, and in Dillon and
Wilmer, *Rebel Women*.

Material specific to Seven
Reid, *Oxford Guide to Classical Mythology*, volume 2, 989-92,
gives a list of the presence of the Seven Against Thebes myth in
the arts from 1300 to the 1990s.

The database of the Oxford Archive of Performances of
Greek and Roman Dramas can be searched for references to
productions of *Seven* from the sixteenth century to the present
day at http://www.apgrd.ox.ac.uk/database.htm. Other useful
databases include the Open University project database for the
reception of classical Greek texts and images in twentieth-

century drama and poetry, accessible and searchable at
http://www4.open.ac.uk/csdb/ASP/database.htm, and the
Eighteenth Century Collections Online at http://galenet.gale-
group.com/servlet/ECCO.

On the legacy of the myth of *Seven* in ancient art, consult the
Lexicon Iconographicum Mythologiae Classicae, under
'Eteocles' and 'Septem'.

To my knowledge there are very few dedicated case studies of
the reception of *Seven*.

Fischer-Lichte, 'Thinking about Origins' (355-60), discusses
Schleef's production of a play featuring a combination of *Seven*
and Euripides' *Suppliant Women*.

Fusillo, 'I Sette', discusses Martone's film *Rehearsals for
War*, which features a production of *Seven*.

Torrance, 'Aeschylus in Cuba', is a study of Arrufat's Cuban
version of *Seven*.

Bibliography

A.W.H. Adkins, *Merit and Responsibility. A Study in Greek Values* (Oxford: Clarendon Press, 1960).

────── 'Homeric Values and Homeric Society', *Journal of Hellenic Studies* 91 (1971), 1-14.

────── 'Divine and Human Values in Aeschylus' *Seven Against Thebes'*, *Antike und Abendland* 28 (1982) 32-68.

M. Alexiou, *The Ritual Lament in Greek Tradition* (Cambridge: Cambridge University Press, 1974).

W. Allan, *Euripides: Medea* (London: Duckworth, 2002).

W.S. Allen, 'The Name of the Black Sea in Greek', *Classical Quarterly* 41 (1947) 86-8.

A. Aloni, 'La colpa di Eteocle. Immedesimazione e straniamento. La fruzione dei *Sette a Tebe'*, in Aloni, Berardi, Besso, and Cecchin (editors) 93-103.

A. Aloni, E. Berardi, G. Besso, and S. Cecchin (editors), *I Sette a Tebe. Dal Mito alla Letteratura. Atti del Seminario Internazionale, Torino 21-22 Febbraio 2001* (Bologna: Pàtron Editore, 2002).

A.M. Andrisano, 'La definizione dello spazio scenico nei *Sette'*, in Aloni, Berardi, Besso, and Cecchin (editors) 125-44.

G. Aricò, '*Crudelis vincit pater*: Alcune note su Stazio e il mito tebano', in Aloni, Berardi, Besso, and Cecchin (editors) 169-84.

P. Arnott, *Greek Scenic Conventions in the Fifth Century* BC (Oxford: Clarendon Press, 1962).

M.B. Arthur, 'The Divided World of *Iliad* VI', in H.P. Foley (editor), *Reflections of Women in Antiquity* (New York and London: Gordon and Breach, 1981) 19-44.

H.H. Bacon, 'The Shield of Eteocles', *Arion* 3 (1964) 27-38.

J.-D. Beaudin (editor), *Robert Garnier – Antigone ou La Pieté* (Paris: Honoré Champion, 1997).

D.W. Berman, ' "Seven-Gated" Thebes and Narrative Topography in Aeschylus' *Seven Against Thebes'*, *Quaderni Urbinati di Cultura Classica* 71 (2002) 73-100.

────── 'The Double Foundation of Boiotian Thebes', *Transactions of the American Philological Society* 134 (2004) 1-22.

────── *Myth and Culture in Aeschylus'* Seven Against Thebes (Rome: Edizioni dell' Ateneo, 2007).

S. Bernadete, 'Two Notes on Aeschylus' Septem' (1st Part: The Parodos and First Stasimon), *Wiener Studien* 80 (1967) 22-30.

——— 'Two Notes on Aeschylus' Septem' (2nd Part: Eteocles' Interpretation of the Shields), *Wiener Studien* 81 (1968) 5-17.

G. Besso, 'I Sette e i nuovi valori eroici delle *Supplici* di Euripide', in Aloni, Berardi, Besso, and Cecchin (editors) 145-54.

J. Boardman, *Athenian Black Figure Vases* (London: Thames and Hudson, 1991²).

E. Bona, 'I Sette negli autori cristiani antichi. Presenza e interpretationi', in Aloni, Berardi, Besso, and Cecchin (editors) 233-56.

G.W. Bond, 'Euripides' Parody of Aeschylus', *Hermathena* 118 (1974) 1-14.

A.J. Boyle, *Roman Tragedy* (Oxford and New York: Routledge, 2006).

A.L. Brown, 'Eteocles and the Chorus in the *Seven Against Thebes*', *Phoenix* 31 (1977) 300-18.

C.S. Brown, 'Odysseus and Polyphemus: The Name and the Curse', *Comparative Literature* 18.3 (1966) 193-202.

L. Bruit-Zaidman, 'La voix des femmes: Les femmes et la guerre dans *Les Sept Contre Thèbes*', in N. Fick and J.-C. Carrière (editors), *Mélanges Étienne Bernand* (Paris: Annales Littéraires de l'Université de Besançon, 1991) 43-54.

P. Burian, 'Zeus Sôtêr Tritos and Some Triads in Aeschylus' *Oresteia*', *American Journal of Philology* 107.3 (1986) 332-42.

W. Burkert, 'Seven Against Thebes: An Oral Tradition Between Babylonian Magic and Greek Literature', in C. Brilliante, M. Cantilena, and C.O. Pave (editors), *I Poemi Epici Rapsodici Non Omerici e La Tradizione Orale* (Padua: Editrice Antenore, 1981) 29-51.

——— *Greek Religion* (Cambridge, Massachusetts: Harvard University Press, 1985) (translated from the 1977 German original by J. Raffan).

A.P. Burnett, 'Curse and Dream in Aeschylus' *Septem*', *Greek, Roman and Byzantine Studies* 14 (1973) 343-68.

L. Byrne, 'Fear in the *Seven Against Thebes*', in S. Deacy and K.F. Pierce (editors), *Rape in Antiquity* (London: Duckworth, 1997) 143-62.

D.L. Cairns, *Aidôs: The Psychology and Ethics of Honour and Shame in Ancient Greek Literature* (Oxford: Oxford University Press, 1993).

——— '*Hybris*, Dishonour, and Thinking Big', *Journal of Hellenic Studies* 116 (1996) 1-32.

——— 'Affronts and Quarrels in the *Iliad*', in D.L. Cairns (editor), *Oxford Readings in Homer's* Iliad (Oxford: Oxford University Press, 2001) 203-19 [revised from *Papers of the Leeds International Latin Seminar* 7 (1993) 155-67].

Bibliography

R.S. Caldwell, 'The Misogyny of Eteocles', *Arethusa* 6 (1973) 197-231.

H.D. Cameron, 'The Debt to Earth in the *Seven Against Thebes*', *Transactions of the American Philological Society* 95 (1964) 1-8.

—— 'The Power of Words in the *Seven Against Thebes*', *Transactions of the American Philological Society* 101 (1970) 95-118.

—— *Studies on the Seven Against Thebes of Aeschylus* (The Hague: Mouton, 1971).

D.M. Carter, 'Was Attic Tragedy Democratic?', *Polis* 21 (2004) 1-25.

G. Chiarini, 'Il ritorno della Sfinge. Immagini e simboli nei *Sette a Tebe* di Eschilo', in Aloni, Berardi, Besso, and Cecchin (editors) 11-25.

E. Cingano, 'I nomi dei Sette a Tebe e degli Epigoni nella tradizione epica, tragica, e iconographica', in Aloni, Berardi, Besso, and Cecchin (editors) 27-62.

A.J. Clark, M. Elston, and M.L. Hart, *Understanding Greek Vases: A Guide to Terms, Styles, and Techniques* (Los Angeles: Getty Publications, 2002).

C. Collard (editor), *Euripides: Supplices* (two volumes) (Groningen: Bouma's Boekhuis B.V., 1975).

D.J. Conacher, *Aeschylus: The Earlier Plays and Related Studies* (Toronto: University of Toronto Press, 1996).

E. Csapo and W.J. Slater, *The Context of Ancient Drama* (Ann Arbor: University of Michigan Press, 1994).

R.D. Dawe, 'The End of *Seven Against Thebes*', *Classical Quarterly* 17 (1967) 16-28.

—— 'The End of *Seven Against Thebes* Yet Again', in R.D. Dawe, J. Diggle and P. Easterling (editors), *Dionysiaca: Nine Studies in Greek Poetry by Former Pupils Presented to Sir Denys Page on his Seventieth Birthday* (Cambridge: Cambridge University Library, 1978) 87-103.

C.M. Dawson, *The Seven Against Thebes by Aeschylus* (Englewood Cliffs, N.J.: Prentice-Hall Inc., 1970).

S. Deacy, 'Athena and Ares: War, Violence and Warlike Deities', in H. van Wees (editor), *War and Violence in Ancient Greece* (London and Swansea: Duckworth and The Classical Press of Wales, 2000) 299-314.

M. Delcourt, 'Le Rôle du Choeur dans Les Sept Devant Thèbes', *L'Antiquité Classique* 1 (1932) 25-33.

P. Demont, 'Lots héroïques: Remarques sur le tirage au sort de l'*Iliade* aux *Sept contre Thèbes* d'Eschyle', *Revue des Études Grecques* 113 (2000) 299-325.

A. DeVito, 'Eteocles, Amphiaraus, and Necessity in Aeschylus' *Seven Against Thebes*', *Hermes* 127 (1999) 165-71.

J. Dillon and S.E. Wilmer (editors), *Rebel Women: Staging Ancient Greek Drama Today* (London: Methuen, 2005).

E.R. Dodds, *The Greeks and the Irrational* (Berkeley: University of California Press, 1951).

K. Dowden, *Death and the Maiden: Girls' Initiation Rites in Greek Mythology* (London: Routledge, 1989).

P.E. Easterling, 'Anachronism in Greek Tragedy', *Journal of Hellenic Studies* 105 (1985), 1-10.

―――― (editor), *The Cambridge Companion to Greek Tragedy* (Cambridge: Cambridge University Press, 1997).

―――― 'The Image of the *Polis* in Greek Tragedy', in M.H. Hansen (editor), *The Imaginary Polis* (Copenhagen: Royal Danish Academy of Sciences and Letters, 2005) 49-72.

L. Edmunds, 'Sounds Off Stage and On Stage in Aeschylus, *Seven Against Thebes*', in Aloni, Berardi, Besso, and Cecchin (editors) 105-15.

R.R. Edwards (editor), *John Lydgate: The Siege of Thebes* (Kalamazoo, Michigan: Medieval Institute Publications, 2001).

C.A. Faraone, 'Molten Wax, Spilt Wine and Mutilated Animals: Sympathetic Magic in Near Eastern and Early Greek Oath Ceremonies', *Journal of Hellenic Studies* 113 (1993) 60-80.

G. Ferrari, 'Eye-Cups', *Revue Archéologique* no. 1 (1986) 5-20.

E. Fischer-Lichte, 'Thinking about the Origins of Theatre in the 1970s', in Hall, Macintosh, and Wrigley (editors) 329-60.

N.R.E Fisher, *Hybris: A Study in the Values of Honour and Shame in Ancient Greece* (Warminster: Aris and Phillips, 1992).

H.P. Foley, *Female Acts in Greek Tragedy* (Princeton: Princeton University Press, 2001).

P. Fornaro, 'Polinice, von Ebrennac e il castigo del silenzio. Come e perché risorge un mito', in Aloni, Berardi, Besso, and Cecchin (editors) 261-80.

B. Fowler, 'Creature of Blood', *Illinois Classical Studies* 16 (1991) 85-100.

E. Fraenkel (editor), *Aeschylus: Agamemnon* (3 volumes) (Oxford: Oxford University Press, 1950).

―――― 'Die sieben Redepaare im Thebanerdrama des Aischylos', in E. Fraenkel, *Kleine Beiträge Zur Klassischen Philologie I* (Rome: Edizioni di Storia e Letteratura, 1964) 273-328.

G. Frank, 'In New York', *Plays International* 21.5-6 (2006) 52-3.

M. Fusillo, 'I Sette contro Tebe dalla scena allo schermo (Su Teatro di guerra di Mario Martone)', in F. De Martino (editor), *Kleos. Estemporaneo di studi e testi sulla fortuna dell' antico* (Bari: Levante editori, 2002) 11-14.

M. Gagarin, *Aeschylean Drama* (Berkeley: University of California Press, 1976).

T. Gantz, 'The Aischylean Tetralogy: Attested and Conjectured

Groups', *American Journal of Philology* 101 (1980) 133-64 [reprinted in Lloyd, *Oxford Readings*, 40-70].

—— *Early Greek Myth: A Guide to Literary and Artistic Sources* (Baltimore and London: Johns Hopkins University Press, 1993).

R. Garland, *Surviving Greek Tragedy* (London: Duckworth, 2004).

A.F. Garvie, 'Aeschylus' Simple Plots', in R.D. Dawe, J. Diggle and P. Easterling (editors) *Dionysiaca: Nine Studies in Greek Poetry by Former Pupils Presented to Sir Denys Page on his Seventieth Birthday* (Cambridge: Cambridge University Library, 1978) 63-86.

M. Giordano-Zecharya, 'Ritual Appropriateness in *Seven Against Thebes*. Civic Religion in a Time of War', *Mnemosyne* 59 (2006) 53-74.

B. Goff, 'The Women of Thebes', *Classical Journal* 90 (1995) 353-65.

L. Golden, 'The Character of Eteocles and the Meaning of the *Septem*', *Classical Philology* 59 (1964) 79-89.

S. Goldhill, *Reading Greek Tragedy* (Cambridge: Cambridge University Press, 1986).

—— 'The Great Dionysia and Civic Ideology', *Journal of Hellenic Studies* 107 (1987) 58-76.

—— 'Battle Narrative and Politics in Aeschylus' *Persae*', *Journal of Hellenic Studies* 108 (1988) 198-93 [reprinted in T. Harrison (editor), *Greeks and Barbarians* (Edinburgh: Edinburgh University Press, 2002) 50-61].

—— 'The Audience of Athenian Tragedy', in P.E. Easterling (editor), *The Cambridge Companion to Greek Tragedy* (Cambridge: Cambridge University Press, 1997) 54-68.

—— 'Civic Ideology and the Problem of Difference: The Politics of Aeschylean Tragedy, Once Again', *Journal of Hellenic Studies* 120 (2000) 34-56.

—— *Aeschylus: The Oresteia* (Cambridge: Cambridge University Press, 2004[2]).

J. Gregory (editor), *A Companion to Greek Tragedy* (Oxford: Blackwell Publishing, 2005).

D. Grene and R. Lattimore, *Aeschylus II: The Suppliant Maidens and The Persians translated by S.G. Bernadete, Seven Against Thebes and Prometheus Bound translated by D. Grene* (Chicago: University of Chicago Press, 1992[2]).

M. Griffith (editor), *Sophocles: Antigone* (Cambridge: Cambridge University Press, 1999).

E. Griffiths, *Medea* (Oxford and New York: Routledge, 2006).

G. Guidorizzi, 'Uno scudo pieno di sangue', in Aloni, Berardi, Besso, and Cecchin (editors) 63-72.

E. Hall, *Inventing the Barbarian: Greek Self-Definition through Tragedy* (Oxford: Oxford University Press, 1989).

—— 'Is there a *Polis* in Aristotle's *Poetics*?', in M. Silk (editor), *Tragedy and the Tragic: Greek Theatre and Beyond* (Oxford: Oxford University Press, 1996) 295-309.

—— (editor), *Aeschylus: Persians* (Warminster: Aris & Phillips, 1996).

E. Hall and F. Macintosh, *Greek Tragedy and the British Stage 1600-1914* (Oxford: Oxford University Press, 2005).

E. Hall, F. Macintosh, and O. Taplin (editors), *Medea in Performance 1500-2000* (Oxford: Legenda, 2000).

E. Hall, F. Macintosh, and A. Wrigley (editors), *Dionysus Since 69: Greek Tragedy at the Dawn of the Third Millennium* (Oxford: Oxford University Press, 2004).

S. Halliwell, 'Human Limits and the Religion of Greek Tragedy', *Journal of Literature and Theology* 4.2 (1990) 169-80.

N.G.L. Hammond, 'Personal Freedom and its Limitations in the *Oresteia*', *Journal of Hellenic Studies* 85 (1965) 42-55.

M.H. Hansen, *Polis and City-State* (Copenhagen: Royal Danish Academy of Sciences and Letters, 1998).

T. Harrison, *The Emptiness of Asia: Aeschylus' Persians and the History of the Fifth Century* (London: Duckworth, 2000).

A. Hecht and H.H. Bacon, *Aeschylus: Seven Against Thebes* (New York and Oxford: Oxford University Press, 1973).

A. Henrichs, 'Anonymity and Polarity: Unknown Gods and Nameless Altars at the Areopagus', *Illinois Classical Studies* 19 (1994) 27-58.

J. Herington, *Aeschylus* (New Haven and London: Yale University Press, 1986).

G. Holst-Warhaft, *Dangerous Voices: Women's Laments and Greek Literature* (London and New York: Routledge, 1992).

T.K. Hubbard, 'Tragic Preludes: Aeschylus *Seven Against Thebes* 4-8', *Phoenix* 46 (1992) 299-308.

—— (editor), *Homosexuality in Greece and Rome: A Sourcebook of Basic Documents* (Berkeley: University of California Press, 2003).

G.O. Hutchinson (editor), *Aeschylus: Septem Contra Thebas* (Oxford: Oxford University Press, 1985).

G. Ieranò, 'La città delle donne. Il sesto canto dell' *Iliade* e il *Sette contro Tebe* di Eschilo', in Aloni, Berardi, Besso, and Cecchin (editors) 73-92.

E. Jackson, 'The Argument of *Septem Contra Thebas*', *Phoenix* 42 (1988) 287-303.

F. Jacoby (editor), *Die Fragmente der griechischen Historiker* (Leiden: Brill, 1923-58 [repr. 1954-69]).

S.I. Johnston, *Restless Dead: Encounters Between the Living and the Dead in Ancient Greece* (Berkeley: University of California Press, 1999).

P. Judet de la Combe, 'Étéocle Interprète: action et langage dans la scène centrale des *Sept contre Thèbes* d'Eschyle', in *Le texte et ses representations* (Paris: Presse de l'École normale superieure, 1987) 57-79.

―――― 'La Langue de Thèbes (Les *Sept contre Thèbes*, 72 sqq. et 170)', *Métis* 3 (1988) 207-30.

R. Kassel and C. Austin (editors), *Poetae Comici Graeci V* (Berlin: de Gruyter, 1986).

G.M. Kirkwood, 'Eteocles Oiakostrophos', *Phoenix* 23 (1969) 9-25.

R. Krumeich, N. Pechstein, and B. Seidensticker (editors), *Das griechische Satyrspiel* (Darmstadt: Wissenschaftliche Buchgesellschaft, 1999).

J.F. Lazenby, *The Spartan Army* (Warminster: Aris and Phillips, 1985).

A. Lebeck, *The Oresteia: A Study in Language and Structure* (Washington: Center for Hellenic Studies, 1971).

A. Lesky, 'Eteocles in den Sieben gegen Theben', *Wiener Studien* 74 (1961) 5-17.

―――― 'Decision and Responsibility in the Tragedy of Aeschylus', *Journal of Hellenic Studies* 86 (1966) 78-85 [= E. Segal (editor), *Oxford Readings in Greek Tragedy* (Oxford: Oxford University Press, 1983) 13-23].

F. Lissarrague, *The Aesthetics of the Greek Banquet: Images of Wine and Ritual* (Princeton: Princeton University Press, 1991), translated from the 1987 French original by A. Szegedy-Maszak.

M. Lloyd (editor), *Oxford Readings in Classical Studies – Aeschylus* (Oxford: Oxford University Press, 2007).

H. Lloyd-Jones, 'Artemis and Iphigenia', *Journal of Hellenic Studies* 103 (1983) 87-102.

A.A. Long, 'Pro and Contra Fratricide – Aeschylus *Septem* 653-719', in J.H. Betts, J.T. Hooker, and J.R. Green (editors), *Studies in Honour of T.B.L. Webster Volume I* (Bristol: Bristol Classical Press, 1986) 179-89.

L. Lupaş and Z. Petre, *Commentaire aux* Sept contre Thèbes *d'Eschyle* (Paris: Les Belles Lettres, 1981).

F. Macintosh, 'Tragedy in Performance: Nineteenth- and Twentieth-century Productions', in P. Easterling (editor), *The Cambridge Companion to Greek Tragedy* (Cambridge: Cambridge University Press, 1997) 284-323.

C. Macleod, 'Politics and the *Oresteia*', *Journal of Hellenic Studies* 102 (1982) 124-44.

M. Manca, '*Frangenda est littera*: l'allegoria dei Sette a Tebe nello Pseudo Fulgenzio', in Aloni, Berardi, Besso, and Cecchin (editors) 219-32.

G.K. Manton, 'The Second Stasimon of the *Seven Against Thebes*', *Bulletin of the Institute of Classical Studies* 8 (1961) 77-84.

D.J. Mastronarde (editor), *Euripides: Phoenissae* (Cambridge: Cambridge University Press, 1994).

G. Mazzoli, 'Giocasta in prima linea', in Aloni, Berardi, Besso, and Cecchin (editors) 155-68.

L. McClure, *Spoken Like a Woman: Speech and Gender in Athenian Drama* (Princeton: Princeton University Press, 1999).

P. Michelakis, 'Greek Tragedy in Cinema', in Hall, Macintosh and Wrigley (editors), 199-217.

J.D. Mikalson, *Honor Thy Gods: Popular Religion in Greek Tragedy* (Chapel Hill: University of North Carolina Press, 1991).

F. Mora-Lebrun (editor), *Le Roman de Thèbes* (Paris: Librairie Générale Française, 1995).

A. Moreau, 'Fonction du personage d'Amphiaraos dans les "Sept contre Thèbes": le "blason en abyme" ', *Bulletin de l'Association Guillaume Budé* 2 (1976) 158-81.

B. Morin, 'La Séquence des Boucliers dans les Phéniciennes d'Euripide (vers 1104-1140): Un Bestiaire Mythique au Service de l'Unité Athénienne?', *Revue des Études Grecques* 114 (2001) 37-83.

J. Mossman, 'Women's Voices', in J. Gregory (editor), *A Companion to Greek Tragedy* (Oxford: Blackwell Publishing, 2005) 352-65.

G. Nagy, *The Best of the Achaeans: Concepts of the Hero in Archaic Greek Poetry* (Baltimore and London: Johns Hopkins University Press, 1979).

M.C. Nussbaum, *The Fragility of Goodness: Luck and Ethics in Greek Tragedy and Philosophy* (Cambridge: Cambridge University Press, 2001² (revised edition [1986]).

B. Otis, 'The Unity of the *Seven Against Thebes*', *Greek, Roman and Byzantine Studies* 3 (1960) 153-74.

R. Padel, *In and Out of the Mind: Greek Images of the Tragic Self* (Princeton: Princeton University Press, 1992).

—— *Whom Gods Destroy: Elements of Greek and Tragic Madness* (Princeton: Princeton University Press, 1995).

H.W. Parke, *Greek Oracles* (London: Hutchinson University Library, 1967).

R. Parker, *Miasma: Pollution and Purification in Early Greek Religion* (Oxford: Oxford University Press, 1983).

—— 'Sacrifice and Battle', in H. van Wees (editor), *War and Violence in Ancient Greece* (London and Swansea: Duckworth and The Classical Press of Wales, 2000) 299-314.

—— *Polytheism and Society at Athens* (Oxford: Oxford University Press, 2005).

C.B.R. Pelling, 'Aeschylus' *Persae* and History', in C.B.R. Pelling (editor), *Greek Tragedy and the Historian* (Oxford: Oxford University Press, 1997).

Bibliography

Z. Petre, 'Thèmes Dominants et Attitudes Politiques dans *Les Sept contre Thèbes* d'Eschyle', *Studii Classice* 13 (1971) 15-28.

R. Pfeiffer, *History of Classical Scholarship: From the Beginnings to the End of the Hellenistic Age* (Oxford: Oxford University Press, 1968).

A. Pickard-Cambridge, *The Theatre of Dionysus in Athens* (Oxford: Clarendon Press, 1946).

M. Platnauer (editor), *Euripides: Iphigenia in Tauris* (Oxford: Oxford University Press, 1938).

A.J. Podlecki, 'The Character of Eteocles in Aeschylus' *Septem*', *Transactions of the American Philological Association* 95 (1964) 283-99.

—— *The Political Background of Aeschylean Tragedy* (Ann Arbor: University of Michigan Press, 1966).

—— '*Polis* and Monarch in Early Attic Tragedy', in J.P. Euben (editor), *Greek Tragedy and Political Theory* (California: University of California Press, 1986) 76-100.

—— '*Kat' archês gar philaitios leôs*: The Concept of Leadership in Aeschylus', in A.H. Sommerstein, J. Henderson and B. Zimmermann (editors), *Tragedy, Comedy and the Polis* (Bari: Levante Editori, 1993) 55-79.

L.A. Post, 'The Seven Against Thebes as Propaganda for Pericles', *Classical World* 44 (1950) 49-52.

A.J.N.W. Prag, *The Oresteia: Iconographic and Narrative Tradition* (Warminster: Aris and Phillips, 1985).

W.K. Pritchett, *The Greek State at War* (five volumes) (Berkeley: University of California Press, 1974-1991).

S. Pulleyn, *Prayer in Greek Religion* (Oxford: Oxford University Press, 1997).

S. Radt (editor), *Tragicorum Graecorum Fragmenta III Aeschylus* (Göttingen: Vandenhoeck & Ruprecht, 1985).

J.D. Reid (editor), *The Oxford Guide to Classical Mythology in the Arts 1300-1990s* (two volumes) (Oxford: Oxford University Press, 1993).

M. Revermann, *Comic Business: Theatricality, Dramatic Technique, and Performance Contexts of Aristophanic Comedy* (Oxford: Oxford University Press, 2006).

L.D. Reynolds and N.G. Wilson, *Scribes and Scholars: A Guide to the Transmission of Greek and Latin Literature* (Oxford: Oxford University Press, 1991[3]).

P. Rhodes, 'Nothing To Do With Democracy: Athenian Drama and the *Polis*', *Journal of Hellenic Studies* 123 (2003) 104-19.

J. Rohou (editor), *Racine: Théâtre Complet* (Paris: Librairie Générale Française, 1998).

H.M. Roisman, 'Dry Tearless Eyes', *Mnemosyne* 41 (1988) 26-38.

—— 'Oedipus' Curse in Aeschylus' *Septem*', *Eranos* 86 (1988) 77-84.

————— 'The Messenger and Eteocles in the *Seven Against Thebes*', *L'Antiquité Classique* 69 (1990) 17-36.

————— 'Women's Free Speech in Greek Tragedy', in I. Sluiter and R.M. Rosen (editors), *Free Speech in Classical Antiquity* (Leiden: Brill, 2004) 91-114.

H.J. Rose, *A Commentary on the Surviving Plays of Aeschylus: Volume I* (Amsterdam: N.V. Noord-Hollandsche Uitgerers Maatschappij, 1957).

D. Rosenbloom, 'Shouting "Fire" in a Crowded Theater: Phrynichos's *Capture of Miletus* and the Politics of Fear in Early Attic Tragedy', *Philologus* 137.2 (1993) 159-96.

T.G. Rosenmeyer, 'Seven Against Thebes: The Tragedy of War', *Arion* 1 (1962) 48-78.

————— *The Art of Aeschylus* (Berkeley: University of California Press, 1982).

V.J. Rosivach, 'Execution by Stoning in Athens', *Classical Antiquity* 6.2 (1987) 232-48.

R. Rutherford, *Homer* (Oxford: Oxford University Press, 1996) [= *Greece and Rome New Surveys in the Classics* No. 26].

S. Scullion, 'Nothing to do with Dionysus: Tragedy Misconceived as Ritual', *Classical Quarterly* 52 (2002) 102-37.

————— 'Saviours of the Father's Hearth': Olympian and Chthonian in the *Oresteia*', in R. Hägg and B. Alroth (editors), *Greek Sacrificial Ritual, Olympian and Chthonian* (Stockholm: Paul Åströms Förlag, 2005) 23-36.

R. Seaford (editor), *Euripides: Cyclops* (Oxford: Oxford University Press, 1984).

————— *Reciprocity and Ritual* (Oxford: Oxford University Press, 1994).

N.J. Sewell-Rutter, *Guilt By Descent: Moral Inheritance and Decision Making in Greek Tragedy* (Oxford: Oxford University Press, 2007).

P. Siewert, 'The Ephebic Oath in Fifth Century Athens', *Journal of Hellenic Studies* 97 (1977) 102-11.

E. Simon, *Das Satyrspiel Sphinx des Aischylos* (Heidelberg: Winter, 1981).

H.W. Smyth (editor and translator), *Aeschylus I: Suppliant Maidens, Persians, Prometheus, Seven Against Thebes* (Cambridge, Massachusetts: Loeb Classical Library, 1922).

————— *Aeschylean Tragedy* (Berkeley: University of California Press, 1924).

F. Solmsen, 'The Erinys in Aischylos' *Septem*', *Transactions of the American Philological Association* 68 (1937) 197-211.

A.H. Sommerstein (editor), *Aeschylus: Eumenides* (Cambridge: Cambridge University Press, 1989).

————— 'The Seniority of Polyneikes in Aeschylus' *Seven*', *Museum Criticum* 30-1 (1995-6) 105-10.

———— *Aeschylean Tragedy* (Bari: Levante Editori, 1996).

———— 'The Theatre Audience, the *Demos*, and the *Suppliants* of Aeschylus', in C.B.R. Pelling (editor), *Greek Tragedy and the Historian* (Oxford: Oxford University Press, 1997) 63-79.

———— (editor and translator) *Aristophanes: Frogs* (Warminster: Aris and Phillips, 1999[2]).

———— *Greek Drama and Dramatists* (New York: Routledge, 2002).

———— 'Violence in Greek Drama', *Ordia Prima* 3 (2004) 41-56.

———— (editor and translator) *Aeschylus I: The Persians, Seven Against Thebes, The Suppliants, Prometheus Bound* (Cambridge, Massachusetts: Loeb Classical Library, forthcoming).

A.H. Sommerstein, A.J. Bayliss, and I.C. Torrance, *The Oath in Archaic and Classical Greek Texts to 322 B.C.* (Nottingham: University of Nottingham, 2007): online database which can be accessed at http://www.nottingham.ac.uk/classics/oaths

C. Sourvinou-Inwood, *Tragedy and Athenian Religion* (Lanham: Lexington Books, 2003).

E. Stehle, 'Prayer and Curse in Aeschylus' *Seven Against Thebes*', *Classical Philology* 100 (2005) 101-22.

D. Steiner, *The Tyrant's Writ: Myths and Images of Writing in Ancient Greece* (Princeton: Princeton University Press, 1994).

G. Steiner, *Antigones* (Oxford: Oxford University Press, 1984).

I.C. Storey and A. Allan, *A Guide to Ancient Greek Drama* (Oxford: Blackwell Publishing, 2005).

O. Taplin, *The Stagecraft of Aeschylus* (Oxford: Oxford University Press, 1977).

———— *Greek Tragedy in Action* (London: Methuen, 1978).

———— 'The Shield of Achilles within the *Iliad*', *Greece and Rome* 27 (1980) 1-21.

W.G. Thalmann, *Dramatic Art in Aeschylus's* Seven Against Thebes (New Haven and London: Yale University Press, 1978).

R. Thomas, *Literacy and Orality in Ancient Greece* (Cambridge: Cambridge University Press, 1992).

I.C. Torrance, 'Brothers at War: Aeschylus in Cuba', in J. Hilton and A. Gosling (editors), *Alma Parens Originalis? The Receptions of Classical Literature and Thought in Africa, Europe, the United States and Cuba* (Frankfurt am Main: Peter Lang, 2007) 291-315.

K. Valakas, 'The First Stasimon and the Chorus of Aeschylus' *Seven Against Thebes*', *Studi Italiani di Filologia Classica* 11 (1993) 55-86.

H. van Wees, *Status Warriors: War, Violence and Society in Homer and History* (Amsterdam: J.C. Gieben, 1992).

———— 'Heroes, Knights and Nutters: Warrior Mentality in Homer', in A.B. Lloyd (editor), *Battle in Antiquity* (London and Swansea: Duckworth and The Classical Press of Wales, 1996) 1-86.

—— (editor), *War and Violence in Ancient Greece* (London and Swansea: Duckworth and The Classical Press of Wales, 2000).

—— *Greek Warfare: Myths and Realities* (London: Duckworth, 2004).

—— 'The Oath of the Sworn Bands: The Acharnae Stela, the Oath of Plataea and Archaic Spartan Warfare', in A. Luther, M. Meier and L. Thommen (editors), *Das Frühe Sparta* (Munich: Franz Steiner Verlag, 2006) 125-64.

P. Vellacott, *Aeschylus: Prometheus Bound and Other Plays* (London: Penguin Books, 1961).

J.-P. Vernant, *La Mort dans les Yeux: Figures de l'Autre en Grèce Ancienne* (Paris: Hachette Littératures, 1998).

A.W. Verrall, *The Seven Against Thebes of Aeschylus* (London: Macmillan and Co., 1887).

D.W.T. Vessey, *Statius and the 'Thebaid'* (Cambridge: Cambridge University Press, 1973).

P. Vidal-Naquet, 'The Shields of the Heroes', in J.-P. Vernant and P. Vidal-Naquet (editors), *Tragedy and Myth in Ancient Greece* (Sussex: Harvester Press, 1981). This is translated from the French original (1971) by J. Lloyd.

—— *The Black Hunter: Forms of Thought and Forms of Society in the Greek World* (Baltimore: Johns Hopkins University Press, 1986). This is translated from the French original (1981) by A. Szegedy-Maszak, with a foreword by B. Knox.

K. von Fritz, *Antike und moderne Tragödie* (Berlin: De Gruyter, 1962), with 193-226 'The Character of Eteocles in Aeschylus' *Seven Against Thebes*', now translated in M. Lloyd (editor) 141-73.

L. Watson, *Arae: The Curse Poetry of Antiquity* (Leeds: Francis Cairns, 1991).

M. West, 'The Midnight Planet', *Journal of Hellenic Studies* 100 (1980) 206-8.

—— (translator) *Greek Lyric Poetry* (Oxford: Oxford University Press, 1993).

—— 'Ancestral Curses', in J. Griffin (editor), *Sophocles Revisited: Essays Presented to Sir Hugh Lloyd-Jones* (Oxford: Oxford University Press, 1999) 31-45.

L.G. Whitbread, *Fulgentius the Mythographer Translated from the Latin with Introductions* (Ohio: Ohio State University Press, 1971).

D. Wiles, 'The Seven Gates of Aeschylus', in N.W. Slater and B. Zimmermann (editors), *Intertextualität in der griechisch-römischen Komödie* (Stuttgart: M & P Verlag für Wissenschaft und Forschung, 1993) 180-94.

—— *Tragedy in Athens: Performance Space and Theatrical Meaning* (Cambridge: Cambridge University Press, 1997).

R.P. Winnington-Ingram, '*Septem Contra Thebas*', *Yale Classical*

Studies 25 (1977) 1-45 [= *Studies in Aeschylus Studies in Aeschylus* (Cambridge: Cambridge University Press, 1983) 16-54].

M. Wright, *Euripides' Escape Tragedies* (Oxford: Oxford University Press, 2005).

F. Zeitlin, 'The Motif of the Corrupted Sacrifice in Aeschylus' *Oresteia*', *Transactions of the American Philological Association* 96 (1965) 463-508.

────── *Under the Sign of the Shield: Semiotics and Aeschylus'* Seven Against Thebes (Rome: Edizioni dell' Ateneo, 1982).

────── 'Thebes: Theater of Self and Society in Athenian Drama', in J.P. Euben (editor), *Greek Tragedy and Political Theory* (California: University of California Press, 1986) 101-41.

────── 'Patterns of Gender in Aeschylean Drama: *Seven Against Thebes* and the Danaid Trilogy', in M. Griffith and D.J. Mastronarde (editors), *Cabinet of the Muses: Essays on Classical and Comparative Literature in Honor of Thomas G. Rosenmeyer* (Berkeley: University of California Press, 1990) 103-15.

B. Zimmermann, 'Coro e azione drammatica nei *Sette contro Tebe* di Eschilo', in Aloni, Berardi, Besso, and Cecchin (editors) 117-24.

G. Zuntz, *The Political Plays of Euripides* (Manchester: Manchester University Press, 1955).

Glossary

Aegis. The apotropaic pectoral shield of Athena adorned with Medusa's head.

Agôn. A contest of any kind. Agonistic competition was pervasive in ancient Greek life.

Anapaest. A metrical form comprised of two short syllables and one long (∪ ∪ —).

Anceps. A syllable which can be either short or long, written ×.

Antistrophe. See **strophe** below.

Aôros, Aôrê. The spirit of a man or woman who had died too young (plural *aôroi, aôrai*).

Apotropaic. That which wards off evil.

Ara. A personified curse (plural *arai*), though not necessarily tied to kindred pollution as an Erinys is.

Atê. A delusion which borders on madness.

Aulos. A double-reeded pipe played as musical accompaniment to Greek tragedies.

Boulê. The council responsible for the daily running of the Athenian state.

Daimôn. An unspecified divine force, or 'controlling power'. The plural *daimones* generally refers to 'the gods' as a collective group.

Deme. A local territory, or village, in Greece.

Dionysia. The 'Great' or 'City' Dionysia was the main dramatic festival at Athens, held in honour of Dionysus, where Greek tragedies were performed. This festival was open to all, including visitors to Athens (though the presence of women is debated). The 'Rural' Dionysia was a smaller-scale affair celebrated by different demes.

Dochmiac. A type of lyric metre expressing excessive emotion (∪ — — ∪ —).

Domos* / *Dôma. Poetic forms of ***oikos***, on which see below.

Dual. A grammatical form designating a pair of objects or persons.

Eisodoi. The long side entrances used by actors and choruses leading into the Theatre of Dionysus.

Ekklêsia. The assembly of adult male citizens who held the decision-making powers in the Athenian state.

Ephebes. Young men, aged about seventeen, on the cusp of eligibility to military service.

Episode. Every subsequent act of a Greek tragedy after the prologue.

Epode. A closing strophe with no corresponding antistrophe.

Erinys. A curse personified (plural Erinyes), also called a Fury, usually brought into being because of kindred bloodshed, and most often the embodiment of a parent's curse.

Genos. One's race or clan.

Iambic trimeter. The metre used to approximate natural speech in Greek tragedy (× — ∪ — | × — ∪ — | × — ∪ —).

Maenad. A female follower of Dionysus possessed and entranced by the god's power.

Oikos. A term designating one's house and household, and also one's kin.

Opfertod. A German term meaning sacrificial death, often applied to such deaths in Greek tragedy performed on behalf of the *polis*.

Orchêstra. The circular dancing area of the Chorus in a Greek theatre, in front of the *skênê* building.

Parodos. The technical term for the entry song of the Chorus.

Pietas. A Roman term meaning sacred duty of various kinds, including filial duties to one's parents.

Polis. The 'city' or 'city-state' in ancient Greece, with all its civic associations.

Prologue. The first act of a Greek tragedy, before the entry of the Chorus.

Redepaare. A German term meaning pairs of speeches, often used to denote the central scene in *Seven*.

Satyr drama. A play performed after a tragic trilogy, whose distinctive features included a chorus of satyrs (half man, half beast), and a preoccupation with sex, competition, and the liberation of the satyrs from slavery.

Sparagmos. The violent dismemberment of a victim completed while in a Dionysiac trance.

Spartoi. The Sown men, sprung from the ground, after the earth had been sown with the teeth of a dragon sacred to Ares. The Spartoi are ancestral Thebans, and their descendants live on in Thebes.

Stasimon. Any choral ode performed after the entry song of the Chorus.

Stichomythia. An exchange in iambic trimeters between two parties where each speaks alternate lines.

Strophe. A unit of a choral song, like a stanza, which has a corresponding antistrophe, a unit which responds to the strophe metrically.

Teichoskopia. Observation from a city wall.

Chronology

Index